INSPIRATION
and AUTHORITY
of the SCRIPTURES

INSPIRATION
and AUTHORITY
of the SCRIPTURES

JIMMY JIVIDEN

Gospel Advocate Company
Nashville, Tennessee

Published by Gospel Advocate Co.
1006 Elm Hill Pike, Nashville, TN 37210
www.gospeladvocate.com

ISBN: 0-89225-545-5

DEDICATION

I wish to dedicate this book to my 10 grandchildren:
Robert, Charissa, Philip, Jama Lee, Jimmy, Paul,
Mackenzie, Jividen, Sarah and Molly.

They are God's children, and my prayer for them is that the torch of truth they now hold will continue to burn brightly in their hands as they participate in the perpetual restoration of the church of Jesus Christ that is revealed in inspired Scripture.

ACKNOWLEDGEMENTS

For the material contained in this book, I acknowledge my debt to many people. Those who read the manuscript and offered valuable suggestions were Les McGalliard, Rocky Whitely, Bill Proctor, Jack Grant, Dale Huff, Edward Myers and Tim Appleton.

Linda Appleton's literary skills in correcting my material made it easily readable and better balanced. Cecil May's help in understanding the doctrine of inspiration and the meaning of technical terms were invaluable. My wife, Shirley, and my son, Steve, helped in the tedious tasks of making clumsy sentences readable and avoiding redundancy.

Phil Sanders' writings on postmodernism were helpful in seeing the influence of this philosophy on the view of the Scriptures held by many in our culture. Greg Tidwell's "Perspective" column in the *Gospel Advocate* has been helpful in showing that a low view of inspiration results in unscriptural innovations. His understanding has been helpful in identifying the underlying cause for the tensions being felt in some congregations.

With so many helpers and such valuable help, I need to say that "we," not merely "I," authored this book.

TABLE OF CONTENTS

FOREWORD

The foundation issue underlying most religious discussion is the inspiration and authority of Scripture. Jimmy Jividen has written effectively on many of the issues troubling the religious world and our own brotherhood in particular, from tongue speaking to instrumental music to fellowship. He cannot have written a more important book than this one.

Convincing evidences exist for the inspiration of Scripture, including fulfilled prophecy and Scripture's amazing unity despite being written in three languages by more than 40 men over a period of at least 1,500 years. The message of the Bible is for many a self-authenticating message because it speaks so eloquently and relevantly to the needs of all mankind.

Not everyone, however, is convinced. Some of the soil on which the seed falls is hardened path, some too shallow and some choked with brambles and weeds. The gospel opens the hearts of the poor in spirit (Matthew 5:3), those who hunger and thirst for righteousness (v. 6), those whose will is to do God's will (John 7:17). When the gospel is heard by that kind of heart, faith is the result. "So then faith comes by hearing, and hearing by the word of Christ" (Romans 10:17 NKJV).

Our faith is foremost in God and in the resurrected Christ, His Son, who reveals the Father to us. But it is Scripture, the God-breathed, written word, that tells us all we know about God and Christ and about their will for us. Because God is all wise and all loving toward us, we believe His Word, and we believe that following the path it sets for us in every detail is best for our lives. It is to that faith that Jimmy Jividen calls us in this book.

The biblical definition of "sound" is "whole," "healthy" and, therefore, "balanced," avoiding extremes. Put another way, a definition of "sound" is "Jimmy Jividen." Like his other books, this one is strong in biblical conviction, careful in scholarship, and firm but kind in dealing with any who may disagree.

A weak view of the Bible produces ambivalence about every truth, challenges the authority of any commandment that is contrary to a present cultural trend, and opens the door to every unauthorized novelty in worship. This book will help establish a strong view of the Bible and its authority and is, therefore, an antidote to many of the ills that presently afflict our brotherhood.

Cecil May Jr.
Faulkner University

INTRODUCTION

Faith in the inspiration and authority of the Scriptures is being questioned in this postmodern world for at least seven reasons:

1. It is done under the guise of defining faith as either an experiential feeling or as a proven proposition.
2. It is done by rejecting the possibility that the Scriptures could be preserved through their transmission from the first century until now without error and corruption.
3. It is done by denying the inspiration of those who wrote the Scriptures. The claim is that those who wrote were only responding to their contemporary culture, and what they wrote is not relevant for contemporary man.
4. It is done by using non-critical hermeneutics that make one passage contradict other passages. This is accomplished by a faulty interpretation of one if not both of the passages.
5. It is done by seeking to make a non-critical interpretation of a passage contradict an unproven scientific theory.
6. t is done by rejecting inspiration, because one with a hard heart and a closed mind does not want to believe.
7. It is done because its teaching threatens the lifestyle one wants to live.

There is a faith crisis on many college and university campuses that were founded for the purpose of teaching the Scriptures along with the arts and sciences. Their purpose was a "Christian" education in which the Bible was regarded as the inspired and authoritative Word of God. But some of these institutions have not lived up to their original purpose.

Many preachers filling the pulpits in the church no longer believe in having scriptural authority for all they teach and practice. The emphasis of their preaching is to please people, promote programs and entertain in worship.

In some churches, this has resulted in controversy over unauthorized worship practices, unscriptural organizations, open fellowship, women leadership and other false teachings. These practices must be challenged and resisted.

A more serious danger underlying these problems is how the Scripture is viewed. Some contend that there is no need for scriptural authority. Others twist the Scriptures through faulty hermeneutics to make them say what they want them to say.

A person's view of the Scriptures, more than any other thing, determines his faith and practice. If the Scriptures are inspired, true and authoritative, then he will have a "thus saith the Lord" for all he believes and practices.

If one's view of the Scriptures is that they are not inspired, not true and not authoritative, then each man will do what is right in his own eyes. It will make no difference what he believes and practices.

The bottom line of any religious discussion is what the participants regard as their religious authority. If it is the Scriptures, the next question is, "How does he view the Scriptures?" How these questions are answered will determine not only what he believes and practices, but more importantly, his eternal destiny.

Jimmy Jividen

CHAPTER 1

BASIS FOR ACCEPTING INSPIRATION

It is a bold leap of faith to accept the Scriptures as the inspired revelation of God. Believing in the Bible goes against the judgments of many leading thinkers – philosophers, psychologists, scientists, politicians and theologians.

Many philosophers put reason over revelation while many psychologists put feeling over revelation. Many scientists put matter and the laws governing it over revelation while many politicians put the favor of the people over revelation. Sadly, many theologians accept academic doubts over revelation, showing more concern with being accepted by their peers than accepting the revelation of God.

Surrounded by such a large and impressive group of unbelievers, many people doubt both the inspiration and the authority of the Scriptures. The idea that there is a God who speaks through the Scriptures is beyond the scope of their academic training and limited experience. They live and think on a different wave length than Bible believers.

The Baptist writer, Harold Lindsell, describes the plight of his denomination in a book he calls *The Battle for the Bible*. He observes that in many seminaries the Bible is no longer taught as the inspired Word of God. Professors in these seminaries double talk, holding onto some biblical terms and concepts while denying the supremacy of Scripture.

A well-publicized division has occurred in the Southern Baptist denomination in recent years over the inspiration of the Scriptures. The American Baptist denomination has long held to a low view of inspiration, denying the truth and authority of Scripture while the Southern Baptists retained a higher view of inspiration, contending that the Bible is both true and authoritative. In recent years, however, a major division over inspiration has occurred even in the Southern Baptist Convention. Similar controversies have happened in other Protestant denominations.

Documenting who really holds to inspiration is difficult because many denominational leaders, seminary professors and popular preachers act like believers in form and confession but in reality are agnostics or atheists in spirit. They no longer regard the Scriptures as inspired.

I do not intend in this chapter to present physical, logical or scientific proofs for the inspiration of the Scriptures. Others have done this and made a good case. My purpose is to show the process by which a person comes to believe that the Bible is inspired.

A MATTER OF FAITH

Faith can bring understanding to that which cannot be known from personal experience or analytical reasoning. The inspiration of the Scriptures is accepted, not by proving a proposition or witnessing a paranormal event that claims to be a miracle, but from choosing to believe the testimonies of qualified witnesses. This was the purpose of John's gospel and his epistles. At the end of his gospel, he writes: "This is the disciple who bears witness of these things, and wrote these things; and we know that his witness is true" (John 21:24 NASB).

The book of First John begins with evidence of John's affirmation of faith: "What was from the beginning, what we have heard, what we have seen with our eyes, what we beheld and our hands handled, concerning the Word of life – and the life was manifested, and we have seen and bear witness and proclaim to you the eternal life, which was with the Father and was manifested to us – what we have seen and heard we proclaim to you also" (1 John 1:1-3).

DEFINITION OF FAITH

Some things are not the same thing as faith. Faith is not an opinion because an opinion is just a personal guess. Likewise, faith is not intellectual knowledge attained by logic and reason. Rather, faith is a conviction based upon the testimony of reliable witnesses.

This truth was first illustrated to me when I was a child. A teacher reached into his pocket and appeared to pull out something held in his closed hand. He asked, "What is in my hand?" I responded with an opinion. I knew it was not an elephant. I knew it was not a red-hot piece of metal. I could respond with only an opinion. It could be nothing, or it could be something that could be held in a closed hand.

He then told me he had a coin in his hand. That seemed reasonable because a coin could fit his hand. He should know what was in his hand because he could physically feel it and open his hand and look at it. He was a reliable witness. I could respond to "What is in my hand?" by saying that it was a coin. That was faith – I believed the testimony of a reliable witness. My teacher then opened his hand, and I saw the coin with my eyes and felt the coin with my fingers. I used sense perception and logic to come to the conclusion that it was a coin. That was knowledge.

The writer of Hebrews describes faith with this statement: "Now faith is the assurance of things hoped for, the conviction of things not seen" (Hebrews 11:1).

Faith is not an experiential feeling within one's own psyche. Emotions are not a valid judge for faith or a confirmation of faith. John warned that one should not believe every spirit, but should try them to see if they are valid (1 John 4:1).

One chooses to believe because of the testimony of people who walked with Jesus, saw His miracles and witnessed His resurrection. This first-hand witnessing was so powerful that those who believed took the good news of Jesus into the entire world although it meant for them suffering, sacrifice and sometimes death. The existence of the church within alien cultures for nearly 2,000 years is a testimony not only of the resurrection of Jesus but also a witness to the Scriptures that reveal it.

The writer of Hebrews said the words spoken by the Lord were confirmed by those who first heard them and who saw the confirmation of them by signs, wonders and miracles (Hebrews 2:3-4). This confirmation was so powerful that the message is still being herald-ed around the world.

One chooses to believe because the biblical testimony fits his soul's quest for fulfillment and the mind's quest for understanding along with his observations from nature.

A HEART SEEKING FULFILLMENT

If a man searches for meaning and purpose within himself, he will find a lonely emptiness in his soul that can be filled only with faith in God. Man's nature is to seek after and grope for God. A God-shaped void dwells in every man. If this God-shaped void is not filled in serv-ing the one true God, then men will make gods and worship objects of their own creation. Without faith one is filled with delusions and doubt. Paul explains, "And for this reason God will send upon them a delud-ing influence so that they might believe what is false, in order that they all may be judged who did not believe the truth, but took pleasure in wickedness" (2 Thessalonians 2:11-12).

Men from all cultures throughout all ages have worshiped something. They seek after and grope for God but cannot find Him because they worship the creation instead of the Creator (Romans 1:20-23).

Discomfort fills their hearts. They desire to know the secrets of their existence, the whys and wherefores of their inner being. Where did I come from? Why am I here? Where am I going? Without the Scriptures, these questions remain unanswered. A yearning for God and a quest for His revelation are within every person.

I have read of an agnostic's dying prayer: "Oh God, if there be a God, save my soul, if I have a soul." He died in doubt still seeking faith and hope. His life was empty, and his hope was futile. Faith in the Word of God brings understanding to the nonphysical, invisible realities within a man.

By observation, one sees the wonder and glory of creation around him and asks, "From whence does all of this come?" The answer comes from the Scriptures: "The heavens declare the glory of God; And the firmament shows His handiwork" (Psalm 19:1 NKJV). This must have been the basis of the faith affirmation made by Paul: "[B]ecause that which is known about God is evident within them; for God made it evident to them. For since the creation of the world His invisible attributes, His eternal power and divine nature, have been clearly seen, being understood through what has been made, so that they are without excuse" (Romans 1:19-20).

God created man with a yearning for his Maker. God made Himself evident to man by making a God-shaped void within his heart. He gave to man a revelation of Himself and His will in the Scriptures. Faith in the message of the Scriptures can fill that void. If that void is not filled with the true God of the Bible, it will be filled with the delusions of men.

Man is astonished by observing the world around him. He wonders at its beauty and is mystified by the laws governing it. Yet he remains ignorant of both the source of creation and the purpose of his own being. Without the revelation of God in the Scriptures, man is in total darkness not knowing who he is, where he came from, or why he is here.

Every effect must have a cause. Without a Creator, there could not be a creation. The Scriptures give answers to these difficult questions. "By faith we understand that the worlds were prepared by the word of God, so that what is seen was not made out of things which are visible" (Hebrews 11:3).

Faith in the Word of God brings understanding to the nonphysical and invisible realities within us.

A MIND SEEKING CONCLUSIONS

Faith in the Word of God answers questions in the minds of men. We want to know who or what is behind our existence and the origin of the world around us. Aristotle and Plato sought to discover the first cause. They reasoned from what they knew by experience and logic and sought to discover the source of it all. They both came to an insurmountable wall beyond which reason could not go. Aristotle called it the "Unmoved Mover," and Plato called it the "Form of the Good." God cannot be discovered by logic or experience.

Anselm of Canterbury (1033-1109) tried to prove the existence of God by reason. He could logically infer that a Supreme Being existed. He failed to show, however, that this Supreme Being was the personal God of revelation.

The presupposition that the Scriptures are the Word of God is the source of faith. Our hearts want to believe, but we must accept the witness of the Scriptures to believe. John and Paul affirm this fact: "Many other signs therefore Jesus also performed in the presence of the disciples, which are not written in this book; but these have been written that you may believe" (John 20:30-31). "So faith comes from hearing, and hearing by the word of Christ" (Romans 10:17).

Man is matter-made and time-bound, living on a small circular mass of matter within a small galaxy of a limitless universe. The mystery and magnitude of it all are beyond understanding. One must confess that someone or something exists beyond this visible physical world in which he lives.

A lack of common sense causes one to believe that something came from nothing or an effect exists without a cause. Beyond scholarly research and scientific experimentation is a reality that must be accepted by faith. This faith begins with the acceptance of the inspiration of the Scriptures. The Scriptures give a reasonable explanation for the universe around us and our being within us.

A SPIRIT MAKING A DECISION

One chooses to believe the Scriptures are inspired because of their own testimony. Their inspiration cannot be proved by scientific evidence or logical reason. Neither can they be disproved by these methods. Faith is based on testimony from reliable witnesses. This faith fits the way the world is and is consistent with reason. It also satisfies the void within the heart of man. Faith in the inspiration of the Scriptures is not produced by reason, and yet faith in the Bible is reasonable.

Reasonable evidence can be given to support a faith decision that affirms the inspiration of the Scriptures. Such evidence is found in both the accuracy of its teachings and the fulfillment of its predictions. The faith that comes from the testimony of reliable witnesses is confirmed by the fact that it has stood the test of time and the ever-changing cultures of man. The Scriptures have endured despite efforts made to destroy them, despite attempts to discredit them, despite those who would twist them to fit the theories of men, and even despite those who simply ignore them. External evidence helps to confirm the faith in Scripture.

• **First,** the Scriptures do not contradict themselves although they were written in three languages by more than 40 men from different cultures and occupations over a period of some 1,500 years. Men allege that contradictions exist, but they have no valid proof. Apparent contradictions can be explained upon closer investigation of the Scriptures and the context. Sometimes claims are made that the scriptural text means something that it does not mean. Sometimes the so-called evidence that is supposed to contradict Scripture is merely an unproved theory that later will be rejected upon investigation.

In 1879, Robert G. Ingersoll, an atheist who was a powerful and influential speaker in the late 19th century, published a book of his lectures titled, *Some Mistakes of Moses*. His lectures drew great crowds. Time has shown, however, that what he alleged to be the mistakes of Moses were in reality the mistakes of Ingersoll. Now it is difficult to find a copy of the lectures of Ingersoll, even in the dusty shelves of a used book store. They have not been reprinted in recent times. In contrast to Ingersoll's once popular book on *Some Mistakes of Moses*, the story of Moses found in the Scriptures is still heralded around the world.

• *Second,* the Scriptures have made predictions hundreds of years before they were to take place. These prophecies were fulfilled in their own time in just the way they were predicted. An often used introductory formula of New Testament writers is that it "might be fulfilled which was spoken" by the prophet (Matthew 1:22; 2:15; 4:14; 8:17; 12:17; 13:35; 21:4). Such predictive prophecies cannot be explained by intuitive guesswork. Isaiah's prophecy of the Babylonian captivity and the return of the Jews to Jerusalem after the predicted 70 years of bondage cannot be a forgery of a later scribe. It is the message of the prophet himself.

• *Third,* the Scriptures tell one story. They were written by men of diverse backgrounds and at different times, yet there is unity of thought and purpose. From the promise that the seed of woman would bruise the head of the serpent to the coming of the Lord in judgment, the Scriptures provide an even-flowing story. The divine plan is revealed portion by portion with each contributing to the whole.

• *Fourth,* the Scriptures are accurate in giving historical information. The sciences of archaeology and history deal with events and cultures of the past. They confirm many of the events, names and cultures reflected in Scripture. Such confirmations are not to be found about other ancient writings.

• **Fifth,** the Scriptures, although written in an age of scientific illiteracy, do not disagree with the scientific discoveries of modern times. Sometimes they were thought to contradict the theories of men, but time has shown either the theories of men to be untrue or the understanding of the scriptural text to be flawed. The Scriptures are neither a scientific text nor an historical book, but when they speak in these fields, they are accurate. God does not make mistakes.

• **Sixth,** the earliest Christian writers after the apostles considered the Scriptures to be inspired and authoritative. Cyril Richardson, in his book *Early Christian Fathers,* says that Clement of Rome wrote around A.D. 96 from Rome to the church at Corinth. His purpose was to heal a schism. He quoted the Scriptures, both from the Old Testament and the New Testament, often and authoritatively. Clement sought to validate his teaching by quoting Scripture. He wrote: "You have studied the Holy Scripture, which contains the truth and is inspired by the Holy Spirit. You realize that there is nothing wrong or misleading written in them (45:1-2)." He refers to the "letter of the blessed apostle Paul" as being "under the Spirit's guidance (47:2-3)" (Vol. 1, 64-65).

A whole body of literature can be found showing the accuracy of the Scriptures. Although these evidences are not the source of believing in the inspiration of the Scriptures, they confirm their accuracy and truthfulness. The Scriptures are accepted by faith, but that faith is a reasonable faith.

FOR DISCUSSION

1. Why do many educated persons reject the authority of Scripture?

2. Some church leaders attempt to prove the Bible's truth through science. What are the strengths and weaknesses of this approach?

3. Describe the differences among knowledge, faith and fantasy.

4. What evidence do you see showing that people in the world are looking for something to give their lives meaning?

5. What implications does a correct understanding of faith have for the work of the church?

CHAPTER 2

A DECISION
OF THE WILL

More is involved than external evidence for either faith or doubt. This is shown when one person comes to faith while another person comes to doubt from reading the same Scriptures.

In the parable of the sower, Jesus taught how the same kind of seed sown on different kinds of soils responds in different ways (Matthew 13:1-9). Seed sown on the good soil bore fruit. Seed sown on the wayside soil, the stony soil and thorny soil did not bear fruit. The seed was the same, but the soil was different.

Such is the case of man's response to the Scripture. The Word of God is the seed, and the soil is the hearts of men. The Word of God in good and honest hearts produces faith. It does not bear fruit in hard and doubtful hearts. The parable ends with the exhortation, "He who has ears, let him hear" (Matthew 13:9). The fruit of faith can come only to those who listen with a good and honest heart. This was the case of Israel in the exodus.

All of the Israelites who crossed the Red Sea died in the wilderness with the exception of the young children and Joshua and Caleb. They died in doubt because "they did not all heed the glad tidings" (Romans 10:16).

The letter Jesus wrote to the seven churches of Asia is preceded by an admonition not only to hear but also to heed the will of God: "Blessed is he who reads and those who hear the words of the prophecy, and heed the things which are written in it" (Revelation 1:3).

A faith response to the preaching of the gospel comes from neither divine intervention nor logical deduction but a decision of the will. The hearer can believe, or he can doubt; he can obey, or he can disobey. Each person hearing the gospel has to make a personal judgment.

In exposing the faith problems held by the readers of Hebrews, the author compares them to the faith problems of Israel in the exodus. "For indeed we have had good news preached to us, just as they also; but the word they heard did not profit them, because it was not united by faith in those who heard" (Hebrews 4:2).

The Israelites refused to make a faith decision and were not allowed to enter Canaan. The readers of Hebrews had come to the point of having to make either a decision of faith or a decision of doubt. This is a personal choice that all must make in reading the Scriptures.

FAITH IS A COMMAND

Faith is a command. Like repentance and baptism, faith is a decision. It is a command to be obeyed, an act of the will. Faith and baptism in the Great Commission are put on equal ground for one to receive salvation. Both are things a person chooses to do. One is an act of the will. The other is an act of physical submission based on this act of the will. Jesus stated both these commandments and the blessings that result from obeying them. "He who has believed and has been baptized shall be saved; but he who has disbelieved shall be condemned" (Mark 16:16).

Faith and doubt are choices of each person's free will; he or she alone must make the decision. Each person alone must bear the responsibility for his decision.

There are, it is true, good reasons to believe. There is a God-shaped void in every man's psyche. Nature and the laws that sustain it cry out for the existence of God. The Word of God reveals His being and His nature. An affirmation of faith is the most reasonable response to the evidence seen in the physical world and the unfulfilled emptiness one feels within himself.

We live in a time when countless theories have been espoused for the origin, scope and nature of the universe. Every theory must take into account that "something was" before "something can be." The scope of the universe is beyond measurement. The nature of the universe is beyond understanding. The origin of the universe is beyond reason. Every theory that leaves God out must deal with the questions of how matter came into existence from nothing, how nature's laws exist without change, and how life originated from dead matter. The physical universe cries out for the existence of God. The Scriptures reveal God and His will for man, satisfying the void within man and answering the questions of existence. The Scriptures answer the question of who or what was before the beginning. "Let all the inhabitants of the world stand in awe of Him. For He spoke, and it was done; He commanded and it stood fast" (Psalm 33:8-9).

There are good and sufficient reasons to come to faith. Faith is a command of God that must be obeyed for one to receive salvation. How, then, does one come to believe? How is the command to be obeyed?

How to Believe

The source of faith is the Word of God. Paul said, "So faith comes from hearing, and hearing by the word of Christ" (Romans 10:17). It is impossible to come to faith without hearing the Word of God. In the same context Paul said, "And how shall they believe in Him whom they have not heard? And how shall they hear without a preacher?" (Romans 10:14).

God is primary in the way of salvation. He initiates and we respond. Without the Lord's invitation graciously presented in Scripture, no one could come to faith. As an individual is presented with the Word of God, there are definite things he or she must do to receive the blessings promised in the Word.

• **Step One.** The first step to faith involves open ears. There must be a willingness to listen. The response of those who heard Stephen's sermon was that they "covered their ears" (Acts 7:57). They did not want to hear. Like the children of Israel in the wilderness, "the word they heard did not profit them, because it was not united by faith in those who heard" (Hebrews 4:2).

• **Step Two.** The second step in coming to faith is for one to possess an honest heart. In the parable of the sower, the seed is the Word of God. Some seed fell upon good soil that Jesus identifies as good and honest hearts of men. The seed bore fruit because it fell upon the good soil of good and honest hearts. If the heart is not good and honest, then the Word of God will not bear fruit. In the same way, Paul shows that those who do not receive the love of the truth to be saved will receive a deluding influence so they might believe what is false (2 Thessalonians 2:10-11).

• *Step Three.* The third step to faith is to recognize the emptiness of the soul. A perceptive person will look deeply into his own soul and see how meaningless and empty life is without faith in God and His Word. He is without God and without hope in this world. There is a yearning for God in every man. To fill this yearning, it must first be recognized. Those people present on the Day of Pentecost recognized this, were cut to the heart, and cried out, "Brethren, what shall we do?" (Acts 2:37). They recognized that they were guilty of rejecting Jesus and calling for His death. They were pricked in their hearts.

• *Step Four.* The fourth step to faith is an understanding mind. Reason is involved. The Ethiopian eunuch was reading the Scripture but did not understand its message. When Philip asked the Ethiopian if he understood what he was reading, his response was, "Well, how could I, unless someone guides me?" (Acts 8:31). Faith is not an irrational leap into the dark. It answers the questions of life and existence. It is a leap into the light.

• *Step Five.* The fifth step to faith is a decision of the will. If one does not hear, does not understand, does not receive the Word of Christ, does not see the wretchedness of His own condition without God, he will remain in unbelief. If he makes a decision of faith, he will accept the Scriptures as the Word of God. John shows that faith can only come to one willing to obey the will of God. "If any man is willing to do His will, he shall know of the teaching, whether it is of God, or whether I speak from Myself" (John 7:17).

While doing doctoral work at the University of Southern California, I came to a better understanding of faith in God and His Scriptures. All of my religious professors were agnostics or atheists. In this context, my faith was challenged. While working through this conflict, I sat down and wrote these words:

I Believe

I cannot know by philosophical speculations, scholastic deductions or pragmatic experience that God exists –
   But I believe.

I cannot look into the remote past to envision blank nothingness, and then see by an arbitrary act of God a chaotic world appear –
   But I believe.

I cannot hear the distant thunder of the voice of God when He said, "Let there be," and there appeared plants and rocks and bees, land and stars and seas, birds and fish and trees as God brought both plan and pattern to the universe –
   But I believe.

I cannot feel the surge of life in the clay made flesh of Adam as God crowned His creation by breathing life into dead matter –
   But I believe.

I cannot fully understand the plan of God, concealed from prophets and hidden from angels, but revealed to us in these latter days. Shem, Abraham, Isaac, Jacob, Moses and the prophets with only a dim vision and wonder foretold God's mysteries, but then God broke into history with His Son, Jesus, to reveal His incomprehensible and immeasurable love. I do not know why or how –
   But I believe.

I cannot prove the wonders of Moses, the signs of Elijah or the miracles of Jesus. Both time and space prevent us from the scientific examination of the valley of the Red Sea, Elijah's fiery chariot in the sky, or the resurrection of Jesus –
   But I believe.

I cannot know why my sins could be covered by the blood of Jesus in one noble sacrifice on a remote hill in

obscure Palestine nearly 2,000 years ago –
    But I believe.

I can not describe with words the love of God who sent
His Son or the constant presence of Jesus in our daily life
or the help of the Holy Spirit He sent as a Comforter –
    But I believe.

Somehow I see, hear, feel, understand and know –
    Because I chose to believe.

I would be untrue to myself and God in heaven to deny
the reality of faith within my soul.

FOR DISCUSSION

1. Review the parable of the sower. How does this parable describe the process of coming to faith?

2. The Bible presents faith as a command to be obeyed. How does this contrast with an understanding of faith as a feeling?

3. What are the implications for the teaching and preaching work of the church that come from the Bible's way of salvation?

4. How can a Christian, understanding his or her own faith development, make himself more effective?

CHAPTER 3

INSPIRED SCRIPTURES, THE CLAIM OF INSPIRATION

The Scriptures claim inspiration for themselves although there is no theological treatise within the Scriptures arguing for their inspiration. They are assumed to be authoritative and are affirmed to be inspired by those who wrote them.

For example, the phrase, "it is written," is used a multitude of times in the New Testament. As an introductory formula to a quotation from the Old Testament, it is used to validate the truthfulness of a teaching.

Jesus used this introductory formula three times in responding to the devil's temptations. He regarded the Scriptures as being authoritative for determining right from wrong. Paul often used the same introductory formula before quoting from Old Testament passages. He recognized them as inspired and authoritative. "[F]or it is written, 'Vengeance is Mine, I will repay,' says the Lord" (Romans 12:19). "For it is written, 'As I live, says the Lord, every knee shall bow to Me, And every tongue shall give praise to God'" (14:11). What the Scriptures said was authoritative for Paul and for his readers.

Peter used the introductory formulas, "It is written" and "For this is contained in Scripture," to quote from an Old Testament prophet to affirm his teaching. "[B]ecause it is written, 'You shall be holy, for I am holy'" (1 Peter 1:16). "For this is contained in Scripture: 'Behold

I lay in Zion a choice stone, a precious corner stone, And he who believes in Him shall not be disappointed' " (2:6). In both cases, Peter used a statement from God revealed in the Scriptures to show the truthfulness and the authority of his teaching.

Jesus Himself said, "[T]he Scriptures cannot be broken" (John 10:35). They still cannot be broken. They are absolute, objective and authoritative. They cannot be changed because they are from God.

Men who wrote the Scriptures used human language, wrote from their own experiences and addressed their message to specific situations, but the Holy Spirit guided them in their writing. Peter explained, "But know this first of all, that no prophecy of Scripture is a matter of one's own interpretation, for no prophecy was ever made by an act of human will, but men moved by the Holy Spirit spoke from God" (2 Peter 1:20-21). Prophecy came from the mouths and pens of human prophets, but what they spoke and wrote was from God. It was neither a subjective interpretation nor an expression of their own will. The apostles who spoke on the Day of Pentecost did so "as the Spirit was giving them utterance" (Acts 2:4).

Paul exhorted Timothy to continue to study the Scriptures. He had been taught them from his childhood, and no doubt had made the faith of his mother and grandmother a faith of his own. He still needed to study the Scriptures because they would make him wise unto salvation, they were inspired, they were profitable for spiritual health and maturity, and they were adequate for every good work. Paul told him: "[F]rom childhood you have known the sacred writings which are able to give you the wisdom that leads to salvation through faith which is in Christ Jesus. All Scripture is inspired by God and profitable for teaching, for reproof, for correction, for training in righteousness; that the man of God may be adequate, equipped for every good work" (2 Timothy 3:15-17).

Paul claimed inspiration for what he spoke and wrote to the Corinthians as shown in his teaching about the Lord's Supper. He said, "For I received from the Lord that which I also delivered to you" (1 Corinthians 11:23). In correcting the problem of women speaking in the assembly, Paul said, "If anyone thinks he is a prophet or spiritual, let him recognize that the things which I write to you are the Lord's commandment" (14:37).

A clear statement concerning inspiration is found in 1 Corinthians 2:12-13. Paul affirms in this passage that his message is from the Spirit of God. Even the words he spoke and wrote were taught to him by the Spirit. Notice the language: "Now we have received, not the spirit of the world, but the Spirit who is from God, that we might know the things freely given to us by God, which things we also speak, not in words taught by human wisdom, but in those taught by the Spirit, combining spiritual thoughts with spiritual words."

The author of Hebrews assumed inspiration of the Old Testament Psalms. He quotes from Psalm 95:7 two times, "Today if you hear His voice, Do not harden your hearts" (Hebrews 3:7; 4:7). In the first passage, the author attributes the words to the Holy Spirit (3:7). In the second passage, he attributes them to David (4:7). The writer understood that, although the Holy Spirit inspired the words, David wrote them.

WHAT IS INSPIRATION?

The word "inspired" is used only one time in the New Testament and is a translation of "*theopneustos*" (2 Timothy 3:16). The literal meaning is "God breathed." A number of passages, however, refer to the Holy Spirit as the source of inspiration (Acts 2:4; Hebrews 3:7; 2 Peter 1:21). The source of inspiration is God; the instruments of inspiration are men chosen by God to speak and write.

Jesus promised His apostles they would have inspiration from God when they gave their defense before judges: "But when they deliver you up, do not become anxious about how or what you will speak; for it shall be given you in that hour what you are to speak. For it is not you who speak, but it is the Spirit of your Father who speaks in you" (Matthew 10:19-20).

The human element does not dim the message, although the vocabulary, language and personality of the inspired men are evident. Paul shows this process: "which things we also speak, not in words taught by human wisdom, but in those taught by the Spirit, combining spiritual thoughts with spiritual words" (1 Corinthians 2:13). He wrote in the Greek language, using many terms no doubt learned in the philosophical school at Tarsus, and a religious vocabulary no doubt learned at the feet of Gamaliel (Acts 22:3). The overriding content and even the choice of words were "taught by the Spirit."

The way in which the Scriptures have been preserved throughout history and made available to us today is fascinating. The transmission of the text of the Scriptures is a human process, the study of which is called textual criticism. It is an important discipline used to discover the purest and most ancient text of the Scriptures. This scholarly discipline can identify scribal errors as well as additions and deletions from the original text.

The study of the original languages is a noble and important discipline, which is able to discover the evolved meanings of Greek and Hebrew words as well as the different shades of meaning the words might convey. Both are helpful in understanding the text.

Thousands of ancient manuscripts and fragments of the scriptural text are available for study. Trained scholars who study them assure us that the text is accurate. The study of the language in these ancient *koine* manuscripts and papyri fragments gives us clear insights into the meaning of words and symbols. We can be confident that the inspired Word of God has been transmitted to our time and place without corruption of its message. Jesus Himself promised, "Heaven and earth will pass away, but My words will not pass away" (Mark 13:31).

Affirming the inspiration of the Scriptures does not mean that autographed copies of the original text have been miraculously preserved and accurately translated. Nor does it mean that all textual problems have been resolved or all word meanings have been totally understood. We must still give heed to the admonition of Paul to Timothy for "handling accurately the word of truth" (2 Timothy 2:15).

Faith and reason come together in handling accurately the word of truth. The affirmation of faith is in His promise that His Word will not pass away. This faith is confirmed by the fulfillment of prophecies and their preservation through the ages despite opposition from those who would destroy it, pervert it and ignore it. The exercise of reason is in discovering and critically evaluating the manuscripts containing ancient copies of the Scriptures. The use of the critical rules of language, context and comparison with other texts enable one to arrive at the most correct understanding of the Scriptures.

FALSE VIEWS OF INSPIRATION

Many false views of inspiration exist besides the blatant rejection of it. These views are based upon redefining the idea of inspiration on one hand and twisting the meaning of Scriptures on the other hand through false hermeneutics.

If inspiration is rejected, the Scriptures become no more than a human book. If that is the case, one has no way to understand the origin and destiny of man, the grace of God, the resurrection of Jesus, or God's will for man. The teachings of the Scriptures would be either ignorant superstition or willful folly.

• *Some call the Scriptures inspired, but by that term they mean only that the Scriptures are the product of men with paranormal religious insights.* They think the Bible is inspired in the same way as the *Koran*, the *Gita* or the *Book of Mormon* claims inspiration. Those who hold to this view believe the Old Testament to be a collection of hero stories first passed down by oral traditions, then recorded by men who wanted to glorify the past and give identity to the Jewish nation. They believe the New Testament to be the product of second-century followers of Jesus who glamorized His life and canonized some of His teachings. For them, Jesus was just another Jew whom the Romans crucified. According to this view, Paul glamorized Jesus' life and affirmed His resurrection in order to make a religion. Such a view can make the Bible an ancient book of intellectual curiosity or devotional reading but certainly not a standard to direct a person's life or give him hope in death.

• *Some call the Scriptures inspired, but they mean that only the passages they define as religious truths are inspired.* Dates, numbers, places and events reflect only the limited knowledge of the writers and are not necessarily accurate. J.W. McGarvey, in his book *Biblical Criticism*, identified another false view of inspiration: "Still another theory ... teaches that the sacred writers were guided by the Holy Spirit in all matters essential to the great purposes of revelation, such as matters of doctrine, morals and faith; but in all other matters they were left to their natural powers, and that therefore they were, in regard to these, as liable to mistakes as other men" (215).

This view of the Scriptures nullifies a part of what has been written. If proponents of this view consider part of the text inaccurate or containing factual error, how can they logically accept another part which cannot be validated by observable facts? This view of partial inspiration considers the Scriptures as containing partial knowledge of poorly recorded events in an ancient culture by prejudiced men.

A more current view of partial inspiration is from the writing of Rudolph Bultmann. In his book, *Myth and Christianity*, he views much of the Scripture as myth. The myth has to be cut away or demythologized from the kernel of religious truth in order to get to the real Word of God called the *kerygma*.

• **Some call the Scriptures inspired, but they mean only that the reader is inspired by reading them.** This is a popular view being taught in many religious seminaries in the United States. A clear statement of this position is given by Krister Stendahl, the Swedish theologian and Harvard professor, in his book, *The Bible and the Role of Women*: "But implied in the fact that the Bible is a testimony to and an interpretation of the Christ event is also the fact that it consists of words of men, contingent upon and determined by historical, sociological, and psychological circumstances. Thus we have in the Bible what is absolute only in and through what is relative. It is the work of the Spirit to make the word of man in the Bible into God's absolute word for us" (16).

Such a view of inspiration nullifies any teachings of the Scriptures that do not appeal to the reader. The focus of inspiration is removed from the text to the subjective and whimsical feelings of the reader. The Bible becomes profane instead of holy. It becomes the words of man instead of the Word of God. It becomes that which is judged by men instead of that which will judge men on the last day.

• **Some call the Scriptures inspired but say the cultural clutter of the first century makes it necessary to reinterpret their teachings.** This is a popular way that the Scriptures are being compromised at the beginning of the 21st century. Those who hold this view would suggest that many of the teachings given in the New Testament are no longer relevant because they are too saturated with the culture of the time in which they were written. Such an understanding makes it easy to reject any teaching that is outside of one's own cultural comfort zone.

This view has been applied to such New Testament teachings as divorce, the role of women, and worship in song. Those who hold this view of the Scriptures would say that the culture was different in ancient times so what was taught then must be modified to fit contemporary times.

• *Some accept the Scriptures as inspired but incomplete in authorizing what may be done in the work and worship of the church.* What the Scriptures authorize one must do, but when the Scriptures are silent, one can do what he pleases.

On this point Martin Luther and Ulrich Zwingli differed. Luther thought the silence of the Scriptures was permissive. That is to say, if the Scriptures do not condemn something you want to do, then you are permitted to do it. On this basis he practiced infant baptism and used instrumental music in worship. Zwingli thought the silence of the Scriptures was prohibitive. That is to say, unless there is Scriptural authority for a practice, it cannot be used. On this basis he rejected instrumental music in worship.

This differing view of the Scriptures separated the Independent Christian Church from churches of Christ. They agree on the first part of the restoration motto, "Speak where the Bible speaks." There is disagreement between them, however, on the last part of the motto, "Be silent where the Bible is silent."

The glaring practices of instrumental music in worship and parachurch organizations are not the bottom-line reason for the fractured fellowship in the American Restoration Movement. The real reason is that men hold to different views of the Scriptures and the way they constitute religious authority.

• *Some accept the Scriptures as inspired but reject some of their teachings as not being essential to salvation.* They suggest that belief in Jesus is essential to salvation, but baptism by His authority is not. Some suggest that worshiping the Lord is essential to salvation, but whether instrumental music is used is not a salvation issue. This teaching flies in the face of the words of Jesus Himself: "Not everyone who says to Me, 'Lord, Lord,' will enter the kingdom of heaven; but he who does the will of My Father who is in heaven" (Matthew 7:21). Who is man to judge what part of Scripture is or is not essential to salvation? God, who sent fire to devour Nadab and Abihu because they offered fire upon the altar of incense that God "had not commanded" (Leviticus 10:1), is the same God who will be our judge. One cannot pick and choose what he wants to make essential to salvation.

• **Some accept the Scriptures as inspired but view them as only love letters and ignore them as also being the perfect law of liberty.** God is a God of mercy and grace – unmerited grace – but He is also a God of righteous judgment – eternal judgment.

Certainly one must treasure the Scriptures that reveal the love of God and His grace: "For God so loved the world, that He gave His only begotten Son" (John 3:16). "For by grace you have been saved through faith; and that not of yourselves, it is the gift of God" (Ephesians 2:8).

One must tremble, however, at those Scriptures that proclaim His judgment: "For we must all appear before the judgment seat of Christ, that each one may be recompensed for his deeds in the body, according to what he has done, whether good or bad" (2 Corinthians 5:10). "So then each one of us shall give account of himself to God" (Romans 14:12).

John, the apostle who emphasized love, is also the apostle who emphasized commandment-keeping: "In this is love, not that we loved God, but that He loved us and sent His Son to be the propitiation for our sins" (1 John 4:10). "For this is the love of God, that we keep His commandments" (5:3).

Mercy and justice must not be pitted against one another. They both describe the attributes of God as revealed in Scripture. If either attribute is left out, then one's view of God is too small.

One's view of the Scriptures determines his religious faith and practice. If he accepts the Scriptures as the inspired Word of God, then they are the source of his faith, the standard for his moral/ethical life, and the pattern for worship and service. If he rejects the Scriptures as being the inspired Word of God, then they become for him the words of men and are of no value in guiding his religious faith and practice.

In fact, the Bible for him becomes a book of lies if it is not inspired. If it claims to be from God and to be the truth, yet contains error, it is dishonest. If it claims to be from God but is only the product of man, it is false. If its claims for truth are wrong, how can it be trusted as a standard of religious faith and conduct?

A statement by Dr. Tim Appleton, one of the readers of this manuscript and a member of the corporate board of the *Restoration Quarterly*, says it well: "Scripture is not to be toyed with. It is not to be twisted and squeezed into our needs, wishes or denials. The subtlest and most common attack of the satanic assault is a subversion of God's Word."

FOR DISCUSSION

1. Why is it important that the Bible claims to be inspired?

2. What are some evidences of human involvement in the writing of Scripture? How does this involvement impact the Bible's claim to be the Word of God?

3. Describe the Holy Spirit's work in producing Scripture. How is this work connected with the Spirit's continued work in the church?

4. How does one's view of inspiration influence his view of creation and evolution?

5. Why do some church leaders claim that the Bible contains errors?

CHAPTER 4

HOW APOSTLES VIEWED SCRIPTURES

The Scriptures themselves reveal much about their nature and purpose. The following passages reflect both the writer's and the reader's view of the Scriptures at the time they were first written and read.

HOW SCRIPTURES ARE VIEWED

Two of the most explicit passages on how the Scriptures are to be viewed are found in the letter Paul wrote to Timothy. In 2 Timothy 2:14-17, Paul states:

> Remind them of these things, and solemnly charge them in the presence of God not to wrangle about words, which is useless, and leads to the ruin of the hearers. Be diligent to present yourself approved to God as a workman who does not need to be ashamed, handling accurately the word of truth. But avoid worldly and empty chatter, for it will lead to further ungodliness, and their talk will spread like gangrene.

Paul stresses the need to avoid wrangling about words and worldly, empty chatter. They are useless and lead to spiritual apostasy. Paul warned Timothy that his teaching was not to degenerate into talk about religious things without substance. They were not to be like those who were "always learning and never able to come to the knowledge of the truth" (2 Timothy 3:7).

Timothy was to be diligent and confident in his teaching because his message was important. He was to handle the word of truth accurately and not twist its meaning into something unrelated to the text. It must be understood in its context (2 Timothy 2:15).

The King James Version translates this phrase as "rightly dividing the word of truth," which focuses on separating the teachings of the Law of Moses given to Israel in the Old Testament from the teachings of Christ given in the New Testament to those who live after the cross.

"Truth" was identified as "the word of truth," not some theology or theory of man. Timothy was to remind them of the teaching found in the word of truth. Jesus spoke a similar thing to the Jews who believed in Him: "If you abide in My word, then you are truly disciples of Mine; and you shall know the truth and the truth shall make you free" (John 8:31-32).

WHAT THE SCRIPTURES ARE AND WHAT THEY DO

Paul stresses again in his letter to Timothy what the Scriptures are and what they do when he states in 2 Timothy 3:14-16:

> You, however, continue in the things you have learned and become convinced of, knowing from whom you have learned them; and that from childhood you have known the sacred writings which are able to give you the wisdom that leads to salvation through faith which is in Christ Jesus. All Scripture is inspired by God and profitable for teaching, for reproof, for correction, for training in righteousness; that the man of God may be adequate, equipped for every good work.

This passage reflects six things about the nature, purpose and use of the Scriptures.

• *First,* the Scriptures are simple enough that even a child like Timothy can know them. His mother and grandmother taught him from his youth. This knowledge of the Scriptures produced faith and godly wisdom in Timothy while he was still a child. The lesson for churches today is clear: Bible bowl, memory verses, Bible classes and correct parental teaching of the Scriptures are important. This training given to children is the basis from which they develop a faith of their own.

• *Second,* the Scriptures are sacred writings. At the time this letter was written, "sacred writings" referred to the Old Testament Scriptures. Peter was later to include Paul's writings as being a part of the Scriptures (2 Peter 3:2, 15-16). The Scriptures are to be regarded as holy (or sacred) like the holy place in the temple. They must not be regarded as a product of human wisdom. They are to be read with reverence, believed with confidence and followed with diligence.

• *Third,* the Scriptures contain teachings that can bring salvation. Receiving its message produces faith (Romans 10:17). Obeying its teaching makes one a child of God (Galatians 3:26-27). Trusting its promises gives hope (2 Peter 3:13).

• *Fourth,* the Scriptures are inspired by God. They are eternal, true, powerful and complete. They reveal the origin and destiny of man. They give a record of God's dealings with man in history and point him to his spiritual destiny. They express the nature and the love of God. No other revelation is needed.

• *Fifth,* the Scriptures can make the man of God adequate or complete. They are essential to spiritual maturity. Peter calls the Scriptures the "milk of the word." Paul refers to it as "solid food." They are nourishment for spiritual growth (1 Peter 2:2). Because of the lack of knowledge, the readers of Hebrews were called immature:

> For though by this time you ought to be teachers, you have need again for someone to teach you the elementary principles of the oracles of God, and you have come to need milk and not solid food. For everyone who partakes only of milk is not accustomed to the word of righteousness, for he is a babe (Hebrews 5:12-13).

Both milk and meat are necessary to develop into a mature follower of Jesus. The immature need milk; the mature need meat.

• *Sixth,* the Scriptures are able to equip the man of God for every good work. Whether he needs to know how to remain moral in a sin-sick world, how to be saved from the fear of death and damnation, how to become a Christian, or how to pray, the Scriptures are sufficient.

They are adequate for every spiritual need of man in all circumstances of life and all ages of time.

THE BIBLE COMES FROM GOD

Other very important passages dealing with the way the Scriptures are to be viewed are to be found in the letters written by Peter. In them, he affirms that the Holy Spirit worked in those who wrote the Scriptures to guide them in their speaking and writing. The idea of the inspiration and authority of the Scriptures was assumed by the prophets and apostles. They claimed that their message was from God.

No theological proofs are given in the Scriptures for its inspiration. It is assumed. Peter describes the process:

> [T]he prophets who prophesied of the grace that would come to you made careful search and inquiry, seeking to know what person or time the Spirit of Christ within them was indicating as He predicted the sufferings of Christ and the glories to follow. It was revealed to them that they were not serving themselves, but you, in these things which now have been announced to you through those who preached the gospel to you by the Holy Spirit sent from heaven – things into which angels long to look (1 Peter 1:10-12).

> But know this first of all, that no prophecy of Scripture is a matter of one's own interpretation, for no prophecy was ever made by an act of human will, but men moved by the Holy Spirit spoke from God (2 Peter 1:20-21).

The prophets did not always understand the meaning of the words they spoke and wrote by inspiration. They made careful search and inquiry but did not always understand their own message. Angels wanted to know the meaning of what the prophets said, but it was hidden even from them. Their prophecies would not be clear until the flickering lights of the prophets were consummated in the blazing sun of the incarnation, the life and the death of Jesus Christ. God spoke in times past by the prophets, but in these later days, He speaks through His Son (Hebrews 1:1-2).

The Scriptures did not come from the subjective feelings or the temporal desires of men but from the Holy Spirit through the voices and pens of God's chosen messengers. There is both a divine side and a human side of the Scriptures. Peter lists two human sources of the Scriptures – prophets and the apostles:

> [T]hat you should remember the words spoken beforehand by the holy prophets and the commandment of the Lord and Savior spoken by your apostles. ... [O]ur beloved brother Paul, according to the wisdom given him, wrote to you, as also in all his letters, speaking in them of these things, in which are some things hard to understand, which the untaught and unstable distort, as they do also the rest of the Scriptures, to their own destruction (2 Peter 3:2, 15-16).

Old Testament and New Testament prophets were inspired. The commandments of the Lord were inspired. The teachings of the apostles were inspired. These make up the Scriptures that reveal the will of God to man. What Paul wrote in his letters was inspired along with the rest of the Scriptures.

THE BIBLE SPEAKS WITH GOD'S AUTHORITY

The apostle John spoke of the nature and authority of the Scriptures in his Gospel.

• *First,* Jesus rebuked the unbelieving Jews because they rejected the witness that God gave to Jesus as His Son. Besides the witness of John the Baptist and the witness of the miracles, there was also the witness of the Scriptures. Jesus fulfilled the prophecies spoken by the prophets about the coming Messiah. When the Jews refused to understand that Jesus had came to fulfill the prophets, He rebuked them saying:

> And you do not have His word abiding in you, for you do not believe Him whom He sent. You search the Scriptures, because you think that in them you have eternal life; and it is these that bear witness of Me. ... For if you believed Moses, you would believe Me; for he wrote of Me (John 5:38-39, 46).

Jesus regarded the Old Testament Scriptures as an authoritative source to confirm His Messiahship.

• *Second,* Jesus answered the unbelieving Jews with Scripture when they accused Him of claiming to be God. He said,

> Has it not been written in your Law, "I said you are gods"? If he called them gods, to whom the word of God came (and the Scripture cannot be broken), do you say of Him, whom the Father sanctified and sent into the world, "You are blaspheming," because I said, "I am the Son of God"? (John 10:34-35; Psalm 82:6).

Jesus regarded the Psalms as Scripture and quoted them as law. What was written He regarded as inspired and authoritative. What was written could not be changed or contradicted. The Scriptures cannot be broken.

• *Third,* Jesus promised His apostles inspiration through the Holy Spirit that He would send to them after His ascension. Three passages in His farewell discourse in John speak of this:

> But the Helper, the Holy Spirit, whom the Father will send in My name, He will teach you all things, and bring to your remembrance all that I said to you (John 14:26).

> When the Helper comes, whom I will send to you from the Father, that is the Spirit of truth, who proceeds from the Father, He will bear witness of Me (15:26).

> But when He, the Spirit of truth, comes, He will guide you into all the truth, for He will not speak on His own initiative, but whatever He hears, He will speak; and He will disclose to you what is to come (16:13).

THE IDEA OF INSPIRATION

The word inspiration is not used in these texts, but the idea of inspiration is clearly expressed in three ways.

• *First,* Jesus was going to send the Holy Spirit from the Father to be the "Helper" of the apostles. Luke referred to the same Holy Spirit as causing the apostles to speak on Pentecost "as the Spirit was giving them utterance" (Acts 2:4). This same Holy Spirit Peter wrote about concerning the prophets who were moved by the Holy Spirit to speak the Word of God (2 Peter 1:21).

• *Second,* the Holy Spirit was to teach the apostles all things and bring to their remembrance all that Jesus had said during His ministry. Paul quoted a proverb spoken by the Lord which is not recorded in the Gospels, "It is more blessed to give than to receive" (Acts 20:35). He gave details about Jesus instituting the Lord's Supper although he was not present when it was done.

• *Third,* the Holy Spirit was to "bear witness of Jesus" (John 15:26) through the testimony of the apostles and by the miracles they performed. Near the close of his Gospel, after recording many of the miracles of Jesus, John wrote that "these have been written that you may believe that Jesus is the Christ, the Son of God" (20:31).

The Holy Spirit sent by Jesus from the Father was to speak what the Father wills, to bring to remembrance the words of Jesus and to bear witness to His identity as being the Son of God. He would do this by being a Helper to the apostles.

THE SPIRITUAL POWER OF SCRIPTURE

One of the clearest statements about inspiration is found in 1 Corinthians 2:12-13. In this passage Paul affirms that his message was from the Spirit of God. Even the words he spoke and wrote were taught to him by the Spirit. Notice the language in the text:

> Now we have received, not the spirit of the world, but
> the Spirit who is from God, that we might know the things
> freely given to us by God, which things we also speak, not
> in words taught by human wisdom, but in those taught by
> the Spirit, combining spiritual thoughts with spiritual words.

The Scriptures are not merely sermons by first-century Christians about what Jesus taught. They are the will of God, the teachings of Jesus, and all the truths that the Holy Spirit guided the writers of the Scriptures to write. They were neither the wisdom of men nor the interpretations of men, but God's Word. Paul stated this truth to the

Thessalonians: "And for this reason we also constantly thank God that when you received from us the word of God's message, you accepted it not as the word of men, but what it really is, the word of God" (1 Thessalonians 2:13).

We do not need to know all the means that God used in inspiration any more than we need to know how Jesus changed the water into wine or the physiological means of Jesus' resurrection. We do know from this passage that God not only used the thoughts implanted into the minds of the writers but also governed the words they wrote.

This is not to suggest that the human authors of the Scriptures used some kind of God-dictated language. The writers spoke in languages they knew, used words and examples from their own experiences, and wrote about real life situations. These things do not nullify the fact that their thoughts, their message and even their words were guided by the Holy Spirit.

Sometimes the prophets did not want to announce the message that God gave to them. Moses did not want to take God's message to the children of Israel in Egypt. He tried to excuse himself. Balaam wanted to compromise God's message. Jonah was an unwilling prophet who tried to run away. Jeremiah was a reluctant prophet because the message he bore was doom to his people. He did not want to prophesy bad news. He said:

> I have become a laughingstock all day long: Everyone mocks me. For each time I speak, I cry aloud; I proclaim violence and destruction, Because for me the word of the Lord has resulted In reproach and derision all day long. But if I say, "I will not remember Him Or speak anymore in His name," Then in my heart it becomes like a burning fire Shut up in my bones; And I am weary of holding it in, And I cannot endure it (Jeremiah 20:7-9).

The prophets spoke for God, not according to their own will or understanding but because they were inspired and spoke the Word of God.

More than 3,808 times the Scriptures speak of God's revealing His will to men. Sometimes it was done through visions and dreams. Sometimes it was through oral words from a burning bush or on a holy mountain. Sometimes it was through words written on stone. Sometimes it was through awesome thunder, lightning, fire, darkness and gloom. Sometimes it was in a still, small voice. Always it was God speaking truth for the benefit of man.

DEFINITIONS

To define clearly all that is involved in affirming inspiration is difficult, but the definition given by Rene Pache, in his book *The Inspiration and Authority of Scriptures*, describes the basic factors that are involved:

> We believe that in the composition of the original manuscripts, the Holy Spirit guided the authors even in their choice of expressions. ... And this throughout all the pages of Scriptures. ... Still without effacing the personalities of the different men (71).

The exact nature of inspiration is shrouded in mystery known only by God. Readers and hearers today look through a mirror darkly because of the limitations of the flesh.

Just as God revealed Himself in the incarnation by becoming man, God revealed His will by the inspiration in the Scriptures. If one can accept by faith the mystery of the incarnation, he can also accept by faith the inspiration of Scriptures by the Holy Spirit.

Kippy Myers in *Redeeming the Times* used as a working definition for the inspiration of the Scriptures this statement:

> One working definition of the traditional view of inspiration is, that mysterious process by which the divine causality worked through the human prophets without destroying their individual personalities and styles, to produce divinely authoritative writings (11). (*A General Introduction to the Bible* by Norman L. Geisler and William E. Chicago: Moody Press, 1986, p. 29).

FOR DISCUSSION

1. How does the apostles' reverence for Scripture serve as a pattern for us today?

2. What does Paul's instruction to Timothy tell us about the training needed by young men entering the work of preaching?

3. What does 2 Timothy 3:14-17 tell us about the work of the church?

4. In what way is the Bible's authority a catalyst for change in our lives?

5. How is the work of God in producing the Bible like His providential oversight of our lives? How is it different?

CHAPTER 5

PURPOSES OF THE SCRIPTURES

The Bible has been used for many purposes, some right and some wrong. Sometimes it is viewed as a holy icon used to protect a person from demons. The Bible is often placed on a table as a symbol of religious devotion, although it might never be read. The Bible is used in court to confirm by oath that the witness is telling the truth. The Bible is used at the swearing-in ceremony of the president of the United States. The Bible is sometimes used to press flowers or to keep a special newspaper clipping, treasured letters or a lock of hair. The real purpose of the Scriptures is sadly often forgotten.

REVEAL GOD AND HIS WILL

The purposes of the Scriptures are to reveal the being and nature of God and to declare His will to man. His word spoke the worlds into existence. His word brought forth the flood in the days of Noah. His word gave the unchangeable promise to Abraham that found its fulfillment in Jesus. God's word thundered from Sinai at the giving of the Law of Moses. By God's word Jesus was begotten, conceived and born of the virgin Mary. God's word spoke from heaven at Jesus' baptism and affirmed Him to be the Son of God. God's word brought forth miracles in the ministry of Jesus. God's word was fulfilled when Jesus died on the cross for the sins of mankind. God's word raised Him from the dead. God's word set Jesus on the right hand of the Father in heaven and made Him King of kings and Lord of lords. The word of God is revealed in the Scriptures.

The purposes of the Scriptures are to be found in the Scriptures themselves. The first three verses of Hebrews affirm that God spoke through the prophets "long ago" and through His Son in these "last days."

> God, after He spoke long ago to the fathers in the prophets in many portions and in many ways, in these last days has spoken to us in His Son, whom He appointed heir of all things, through whom also He made the world. And He is the radiance of His glory and the exact representation of His nature, and upholds all things by the word of His power (Hebrews 1:1-3).

This passage describes the nature of God and His desire to reveal His will to man. His will was revealed to the patriarchs, Moses and the prophets through angels (Acts 7:53; Galatians 3:19; Hebrews 2:2). In these last days, God has spoken through His Son. His will was confirmed by those who heard the Lord, and God bore witness to their message by miracles. The writer of Hebrews affirms this process:

> For if the word spoken through angels proved unalterable, and every transgression and disobedience received a just recompense, how shall we escape if we neglect so great a salvation? After it was at the first spoken through the Lord, it was confirmed to us by those who heard, God also bearing witness with them, both by signs and wonders and by various miracles and by gifts of the Holy Spirit according to His own will (Hebrews 2:2-4).

The revelation of the nature and will of God is hidden from those who do not know the Scriptures. They walk in spiritual darkness. Paul shows how failure to honor God and give Him thanksgiving led to the ignorance of God which in turn led to pagan idolatry.

> For even though they knew God, they did not honor Him as God, or give thanks: but they became futile in their specu-

lations, and their foolish heart was darkened. Professing to be wise, they became fools, and exchanged the glory of the incorruptible God for an image in the form of corruptible man and of birds and four-footed animals and crawling creatures (Romans 1:21-23).

The word of God revealed in the gospel reveals the nature and will of God and brought light into such pagan darkness.

[T]he god of this world has blinded the minds of the unbelieving, that they might not see the light of the gospel of the glory of Christ, who is the image of God. ... For God, who said, "Light shall shine out of darkness," is the One who has shone in our hearts to give the light of the knowledge of the glory of God in the face of Christ (2 Corinthians 4:4, 6).

The Jews, having only the Old Testament Scriptures, had a limited knowledge of God's nature and will. Prophets searched carefully and made inquiry into their limited revelation but still did not understand the revelation from God concerning the coming of Jesus. Even angels did not know the time or the means of the coming Savior (1 Peter 1:10-12).

As God made light come out of darkness on the first day of creation, so God brought light out of the darkness of ignorance and sin. He revealed Himself through His Son Jesus and revealed His will through the Holy Spirit.

SEEKERS AFTER GOD

The world before Jesus' coming knew only a hidden God. He was unknown to pagan idol worshipers, unknown to the Greek philosophers, and not clearly known even by His chosen people, the Jews.

When Paul preached the gospel in Athens, he saw an inscription to an "unknown god" (Acts 17:23). The city was filled with idols of every kind, all of which were worshiped as gods. The Athenians really did not know the true God. To them He was an unknown God.

The Greek philosophers were brilliant men who sought to find the causes and consequences of all things. In many physical areas they succeeded. They planted the seed of thought for the development of the scientific method used in problem-solving today. They could not, however, by their reasoning find the hidden God who brought matter into existence, formed life out of matter, and gave spirit to man. The beginning of reason for Aristotle was the hypothetical "unmoved mover." The source of existence for Plato was the theoretical "form of the good." They asked questions dealing with the first cause but found no answer. The answer came when God revealed Himself through His only Son and sent the Holy Spirit to reveal His will in the Scriptures.

The children of Abraham, the nation of Israel, God's chosen people, only slightly knew God. They had Moses and the prophets by which God revealed much of Himself. They heard His voice from Sinai but could not see Him. They knew the story of creation, of Abraham and the patriarchs, and God's actions in history. They did not know God's mystery kept secret from the foundations of the earth. He did not, however, reveal Himself or His will completely until the incarnation of Jesus and the coming of the Holy Spirit. John spoke of this saying, "No man has seen God at any time; the only begotten God, who is in the bosom of the Father, He has explained Him" (John 1:18); and again John wrote, "But the Helper, the Holy Spirit, whom the Father will send in My name, He will teach you all things, and bring to your remembrance all that I said to you" (14:26).

Jesus revealed the nature of God through the incarnation, and the Holy Spirit revealed His will through the Scriptures.

Followers of the mystery religions in the Greek and Roman cultures of the first century sought to find God through experiencing the divine within themselves. These religious experiences were sought in different ways. At the Greek oracles in Delphi, some sought a religious experience through *glossolalia*. They believed their ecstatic speech was a message from the gods. At Corinth, some sought a religious experience by being joined to a sacred temple prostitute in the Aphrodite cult. In the cult of Dionysus, the god of wine, members of this cult sought a religious experience through intoxication. When the spirit of the wine overcame the mind, they thought the god was in them.

These mystery religions seem to have had one thing in common, an emotional experience that cult members identified as having fellowship with the gods. The tragedy of it all was that they were deceiving themselves into believing that this emotional experience somehow united them with their gods. In reality, they were only manipulating their emotions. You cannot find God in *glossolalia*, the sexual experience, drunkenness or a psychological experience. You cannot know God by scholastic deductions, philosophical reasoning or subjective experiences. God revealed Himself in His Son and His will in the Scriptures.

ANALOGIES SHOWING PURPOSES

Many purposes of the Scriptures can be identified by the analogies found in the Scriptures themselves.

• **The Scriptures are the seed of the kingdom, the Word of God.** The soil of a man's heart can receive or reject the Word of God. Jesus said, the "seed is the word of God" (Luke 8:11). Romans 1:16 says the gospel is the source of faith. It is the begetting power of the new birth. Peter wrote that "you have been born again not of seed which is perishable but imperishable, that is, through the living and abiding word of God" (1 Peter 1:23).

The Scriptures are the mirror of the soul. They reflect the secret thoughts of the inner man. They expose one's inner desires just as God sees them. This reflection of the inner man must not be put aside and forgotten but must be remembered and acted upon. "For if anyone is a hearer of the word and not a doer, he is like a man who looks at his natural face in a mirror; for once he has looked at himself and gone away, he has immediately forgotten what kind of person he was" (James 1:23-24).

This exposure of man's inner self must be taken seriously, because it reveals the ugly and the beautiful. When one sees himself as he really is and does not like what he sees, he needs to change. When the Scriptures reveal one's inner self as ugly, he needs to realize that God sees him like this also. He must not forget what the mirror of the Word of God reflects in his own life.

• **The Scriptures are food to nourish and mature the spiritual man.** They serve both as milk for the immature and meat for the mature. This analogy is used by Peter, Paul and the writer of Hebrews:

> [L]ike newborn babes, long for the pure milk of the word,
> that by it you may grow in respect to salvation (1 Peter 2:2).

And I, brethren, could not speak to you as to spiritual men, but as to men of flesh, as to babes in Christ. I gave you milk to drink, not solid food; for you were not yet able to receive it (1 Corinthians 3:1-2).

For though by this time you ought to be teachers, you have need again for some one to teach you the elementary principles of the oracles of God, and you have come to need milk and not solid food. For every one who partakes only of milk is not accustomed to the word of righteousness, for he is a babe (Hebrews 5:12-13).

A person cannot grow spiritually without the milk and meat of the Word of God. It builds faith, gives directions for moral and ethical conduct, reveals the gospel, encourages the fainthearted, exposes sin, and gives hope. To the one who hears, believes and obeys, the Scriptures become the source of spiritual growth. Without this nourishment, one cannot mature in Christ. Daily Bible reading and regular Bible study produce spiritual maturity and health.

• *The Scriptures are the law of liberty.* They are contrasted with the Law given to Moses. That law exposed sin and brought spiritual death. The law of liberty given by Christ freed men from the law of sin and death.

The Law of Moses was good for its purpose, to reveal the sinfulness of man. Paul said that "through the Law comes the knowledge of sin" (Romans 3:20). He also said, "where there is no law, neither is there violation" (4:15). The law made man conscious of sin. Paul further stated, "the Law came in that the transgression might increase" (5:20). The Law of Moses revealed sin, but the blood offerings of animals could not take away sin. The writer of Hebrews said, "For it is impossible for the blood of bulls and goats to take away sins" (Hebrews 10:4). The Scriptures are called the law of liberty because only they reveal God's plan for a man to be set free from sin and the fear of death. Real forgiveness could come only through the sacrifice of Jesus Christ.

Paul said, "For the law of the Spirit of life in Christ Jesus has set you free from the law of sin and death" (Romans 8:2). Sin exposed by the Law of Moses is atoned for and forgiven in the death of Jesus Christ when one experiences a new birth in baptism (6:4-6). The Christian lives under the law of Christ and is admonished: "So speak and so act, as those who are to be judged by the law of liberty" (James 2:12). The Scriptures contain both the Law of Moses and the law of Christ. The Law of Moses exposes sin and brings a person into the bondage to sin and death. The law of liberty given by Christ frees a person from the bondage of sin and death. A person who lives under the law of liberty follows the law from a higher motive than fear of judgment. He follows it because he desires to please Him who set him free. Paul said, "But now we have been released from the Law, having died to that by which we were bound, so that we serve in newness of the Spirit and not in oldness of the letter" (Romans 7:6).

• **The Scriptures, the Word of God, are described as the "sword of the Spirit."** They are the offensive weapon in the Christian's armor:

> Stand firm ... taking up the shield of faith with which you will be able to extinguish all the flaming missiles of the evil one. And take the helmet of salvation, and the sword of the Spirit, which is the word of God (Ephesians 6:14, 16-17).

> For the word of God is living and active and sharper than any two-edged sword, and piercing as far as the division of soul and spirit, of both joints and marrow, and able to judge the thoughts and intentions of the heart (Hebrews 4:12).

A soldier used his sword to fight the enemy. Jesus used the sword of the Spirit when He was tempted by the devil (Matthew 4:1-10). He responded to the devil's temptations by saying, "It is written," and quoting from the Scriptures. Paul used the sword of the Spirit in resisting false teachers. Philip used the sword of the Spirit when he taught the eunuch about Jesus.

• **The Scriptures, the Word of God, are described as truth.** Jesus said, "Thy word is truth" (John 17:17). Paul exhorted the young preacher Timothy when he said, "Be diligent to present yourself approved to God as a workman who does not need to be ashamed, handling accurately the word of truth" (2 Timothy 2:15). The Bereans were commended by Paul for being so receptive to the gospel. Luke records:

Now these [the Bereans] were more noble-minded than those
in Thessalonica, for they received the word with great eagerness, examining the Scriptures daily, to see whether these
things were so (Acts 17:11).

They were commended because they used the Scriptures as a standard of truth. They wanted to know if what Paul taught was in accor-
dance with the Old Testament Scriptures. Jesus promised to send the
Holy Spirit to "guide [the apostles] into all the truth" (John 16:13).
They wrote and spoke "as the Spirit was giving them utterance" (Acts
2:4). They wrote by inspiration.

Time bears witness to the truthfulness of the Scriptures. Science, history, geography and prophecy all bear witness to the fact that the
Scriptures are true and accurate.

• *The Scriptures, the Word of God, are described as a light.* David
said, "Thy word is a lamp to my feet, And a light to my path" (Psalm
119:105). Peter described the prophetic words as a "lamp shining in
a dark place, until the day dawns and the morning star arises in your
hearts" (2 Peter 1:19). While the prophets gave predictions about the
coming of Jesus and the glory of His kingdom, they did not understand
all that they wrote. Peter's language about a light in a dark place sug-
gests that although this light was not clear and bright, it gave Abraham
the hope that his descendants would become as numerous as the stars
of heaven and the sand on the seashore. It was the dim light of the
Scriptures that promised David his seed would sit on the throne of God
(Acts 2:29-31).

Without the Scriptures, man would be in the darkness of ignorance
concerning the origin of the universe, the creation of man, all moral
and ethical standards, the nature and purposes of God, God's will for
man on moral and ethical conduct, as well as man's final destiny. Without
the light of God's Word, we would live "having no hope and without
God in the world" (Ephesians 2:12).

The light of the Word of God is basic to understanding Jesus as the
light of the world. The Scriptures bear witness to Jesus. Jesus told
the Jews who rejected Him: "And you do not have His word abiding
in you, for you do not believe Him whom He sent. You search the

Scriptures, because you think that in them you have eternal life; and it is these that bear witness of Me" (John 5:38-39).

To reject Jesus is to reject the Word of God. To reject the Word of God is to reject Jesus. Jesus said of His own rejection:

> And this is the judgment, that the light is come into the world, and men loved the darkness rather than the light; for their deeds were evil. For everyone who does evil hates the light, and does not come to the light, lest his deeds should be exposed. But he who practices the truth comes to the light, that his deeds may be manifested as having been wrought in God (John 3:19-21).

• *Finally, the Scriptures are able to make the man of God adequate and equip him for every good work.* The Scriptures reveal God's will to man, produce faith in the good and honest heart, expose the sin in one's life, instruct one how to be reconciled to God, and fill the soul with hope of eternal salvation. These same Scriptures will be the basis for judgment on the last day. Understanding the eternal nature of God's Word and its power, man stands in awe and bows in humble submission because it is the only way to know his Maker.

FOR DISCUSSION

1. What do you think about the use of the Bible for non-religious purposes?

2. How is philosophical speculation about God different from God's revelation of Himself through Scripture?

3. How are the pagan mystery religions of antiquity similar to the community church movement of today?

4. What was the purpose of the Law of Moses? How is the gospel of Christ different from it?

5. How is our relationship with Jesus dependent upon the Bible?

CHAPTER 6

THE AUTHORITY OF THE SCRIPTURES

No other doctrine is being questioned or compromised more than the inspiration and authority of the Scriptures. Some question the inspiration and authority of the Scriptures directly, such as those involved in the Jesus Seminar, a gathering of a group of scholars whose purpose is to revise the Biblical account of the life of Jesus with unfounded speculations. They deny the truth of the scriptural accounts and seek to show that they are the product of some of Jesus' followers who glamorized His life and teachings.

A number of TV and movie presentations on the theme of the origin and development of Christianity portray Jesus as a great teacher but seek to show that the Scriptures were the product of Jesus' followers trying to relate the story of Jesus to different cultures. The gospel writers, they contend, did not give an accurate account of Jesus of Nazareth but interpreted the life of Jesus in such a way as to appeal to different cultures of the time. Paul is said to be the one who brought the stories of Jesus together to make them into a religion. The Scriptures, instead of being a dependable account of the life and teachings of Jesus and the development of the early church, were an attempt to relate the Jesus story to the times. This undermines the inspiration and authority of the Scripture by making it the product of men.

Generally this questioning of the inspiration and authority of the Scriptures is not made directly but is clothed in technical, academic or religious language that redefines the common religious words of faith. The meanings of words are changed in order to find acceptance with those who read and hear. Those who question the authority of the Scriptures sometimes use words that, at first glance, seem to affirm them. The meaning they give to the words of affirmation in reality denies the Bible's authority.

THE CLAIM OF THE SCRIPTURES

Affirming the inspiration of Scripture involves accepting by faith that they were given by God through men inspired by the Holy Spirit. The Scriptures themselves make such a claim. Peter wrote in 2 Peter 1:21: "[N]o prophecy was ever made by an act of human will, but men moved by the Holy Spirit spoke from God." And Paul wrote to Timothy saying, "All Scripture is inspired by God" (2 Timothy 3:15).

If one believes in the authority of the Scriptures, he accepts by faith that they are the only and the final standard for religious faith and practice. Jesus said, "Thy word is truth" (John 17:17), and the "Scriptures cannot be broken" (10:35).

Jesus and the apostles quoted Scripture as authority for both affirming truth and resisting sin and error. They accepted the Scriptures as being religious authority.

Those who question the authority of the Scriptures regard them as uninspired religious books handed down from the past, written by men and full of errors and contradictions. As such, they are not worthy to be regarded as religious authority. Nonbelievers seek to undermine faith in the Scriptures by suggesting such arguments as the following: "They are shrouded with all of the ignorance and superstition of an ancient culture." "They are just another holy book among the holy books of different world religions." "They are religious literature from ancient wise men and prophets who speculated about the spiritual aspect of man." "They are not to be taken literally."

The Scriptures are none of the above. They are rather the will of God revealed to inspired men who wrote them.

A new kind of unbelief now questions the authority of the Scriptures.

Its adherents include some with leadership roles in the church. These men use language claiming to believe in the inspiration of the Scriptures, but the way they speak of them leaves questions about both their inspiration and authority.

Religious apathy and compromise was rampant during the period of the judges, because the Word of God given through Moses was ignored in apathy and compromised with culture. The guiding principle for Israel became: "[E]veryone did what was right in his own eyes" (Judges 21:25).

A similar situation exists in our culture today under the fluid term of "postmodernism." This system of thought claims there are no absolutes. Truth is relative. My truth might not be your truth. The Scriptures, because of this way of thinking, are too often ignored in apathy or adapted to the culture. The Bible is no longer regarded as the absolute religious authority. God's Word, as in the period of the judges, is either compromised or ignored. We face an urgent need to return to the Scriptures. The old axiom, "Back to the Bible," is still relevant. This restoration principle can be actualized only when one believes that the Scriptures are inspired and authoritative. The Scriptures must be understood as God-given, inspired by the Holy Spirit, and the final and complete standard of religious authority. God has spoken through His Word.

THE CHOICE OF FAITH

Faith in the authority of the Scriptures is a personal choice. One chooses whether to believe God's Word is revealed in the Scriptures or to reject it as it being just another religious composition of man. This choice is not based upon a better-felt-than-told experience. It is a decision of the will that does not come solely from logical deductions but is a personal choice. It is not an irresistible conformity to contemporary culture. It is an independent decision. One chooses to believe or not to believe. The answer lies in the "will." Unwillingness to do God's will leaves one in a state of doubt.

Paul called upon the jailor to make a personal choice. He commanded him, "Believe in the Lord Jesus" (Acts 16:31). He could believe or not believe. The choice was determined by his will, his mind and his heart.

After Paul spoke the word of the Lord to him, he chose to believe. There had to be the desire of the heart and the understanding of the mind; only then was the choice of the will possible.

Belief in the authority of the Scriptures is not because of a different feeling or an overwhelming experience although one's life is different because he chooses to believe. One does not come to belief because of logical deduction although he finds that his faith fits what he knows of the world, logic and living. His faith does not rest upon the changing culture of men or the passing ages of time. His faith comes from a willful, personal decision confirmed by valid evidences.

The source of faith in either God or His Word comes from a personal choice that an individual makes when he hears the Word of God. Paul said, "So faith comes from hearing, and hearing by the word of Christ" (Romans 10:17).

SUPPORTING EVIDENCE

Faith in the authority of the Scriptures is not an unscientific shot in the dark. It is supported by evidence. Physical evidences of history, archaeology and science confirm Bible history where valid evidence is available.

Faith in the inspiration and authority of the Scriptures is more than a naive leap into the unknown. A person cannot ignore the evidence that many of the Old Testament prophecies, given hundreds of years before their time of fulfillment, were accurately fulfilled in the events of history.

Faith in the inspiration of the Scriptures is not some irrational conclusion. The contents of the Scriptures are evidence for faith. How could some 40 different men scattered in different countries, living in different centuries and under different cultures write in three languages over a period of 3,000 years and yet write one story without contradiction? Inspiration is the only reasonable explanation. These facts give evidence that the Scriptures were written by holy men of God who were moved by the Holy Spirit (2 Peter 1:21).

Jesus called the Word of God "truth" (John 17:17). Paul called the Word of God "holy" and "sacred" (Romans 1:2; 2 Timothy 3:15). If a man cannot accept this view of the Scriptures, he cannot logically maintain faith in Jesus Christ. Faith in Jesus comes by the Word of God. If the Scriptures cannot be totally trusted, then faith in Jesus is based on a delusion. If the foundation is gone, the superstructure collapses.

ATTITUDES THAT UNDERMINE FAITH

Belief in the inspiration and authority of the Scriptures is currently being undermined by God substitutes. The High and Holy God revealed in the Scriptures is incompatible with what most men want to do and with the god most men want to worship.

A definition of "god" in the field of psychology of religion is "the object of ultimate concern." The God revealed in Scripture is not the object of ultimate concern for most men. Most serve idols of their own making, like the pagan gods worshiped by the Greeks and Romans of the first century.

The god of secularism is worshiped by those who make physical things into a god. Secular values become their objects of ultimate concern. The Scriptures expose these values as an idol. Jesus said, "You cannot serve God and mammon" (Matthew 6:24). When one makes secularism the object of ultimate concern, he cannot find fulfillment. His god will not last, and certainly it gives no hope (1 John 2:15-17). If a person makes secularism the object of his ultimate concern he, like foolish pagans, becomes an idol worshiper.

The negative god of atheism makes a religion of rejecting God all together. Believing that there is no God, an atheist has made his denial of God the object of his ultimate concern. His plight is described in the Psalms: "The fool has said in his heart, 'There is no God.' They are corrupt, they have committed abominable deeds; There is no one who does good" (Psalm 14:1).

The atheist has no basis for morality, no knowledge of the source of his existence, and no motive for kindness or spiritual values. He does not believe in God or the Scriptures that reveal God. This person sees himself forced into existence and dumped into an evil, alien world with no hope of heaven and no fear of hell.

There is the god of "egoalatry" – the deification of one's own ego. This man sees himself as the center of the universe. Truth is what is true to him. Right is what he wants to do. Sin is what he does not like to do. Salvation is doing his own thing. Grace is rejecting any personal accountability for his conduct. These beliefs are popular in today's cultures. Followers of this idol reject the Scriptures as religious authority and believe only in values that seem right in their own eyes. Scriptures call this doctrine of postmodernism foolish: "The way of the fool is right in his own eyes" (Proverbs 12:15). One who serves this idol is a worshiper of himself, the object of his ultimate concern.

There is another god of one's own emotion. Most evangelical religions are experiential, that is, a person's faith comes by or is associated with an emotional, psychological experience. With variations, this is a fundamental teaching of most Calvinists, Pentecostals, Mormons and Charismatics. They interpret their own feelings as being their private religious authority and claim that God has revealed Himself through such an experience. It matters not whether this experience has Scriptural support. The personal experience is interpreted as being a sign from God. Emotions are the foundation of this religion and become the object of ultimate concern.

Another challenge to the inspiration and authority of the Scriptures is of the greatest concern. The Scriptures are being questioned not openly but by subtle suggestions. One person might refuse to believe the Scriptures because he thinks they are outdated. Another might reject the inspiration of the Scriptures because he has been told and has come to believe that they are the product of an ignorant, ancient culture and are irrelevant in today's world. Still another might call them inspired but mean something different. The meaning they give to "inspired" does not mean the Scriptures are true, absolute and authoritative. They define "inspired" as being inspirational to the reader. The Scriptures are called inspired because they contain the Word of God not because they are the Word of God. This person believes the Scriptures are inspired but must be re-interpreted in the contemporary culture. The authority of the Scriptures is found to be no more than what the believer wants to believe.

The statement of this view of the Scriptures was given by Stendahl in *Bible and the Role of Women*: "Thus we have in the Bible what is absolute only in and through what is relative. It is the work of the Spirit to make the word of man in the Bible into God's absolute word to us" (16). Because the inspiration is in the reader, the text may mean different things to different people.

These views of the Scriptures and the flawed interpretations of the Scriptures have already brought about apostasy in many churches and destroyed the faith of countless Christians.

Again let it be said, "No other doctrine is being called into question more than the inspiration and authority of the Scriptures."

NEW HERMENEUTICAL CHALLENGES

Four new, but not so new, hermeneutical challenges currently face leaders of the church. These challenges arise from the way Scripture is viewed. Either the Scriptures are inspired and authoritative or they are of human origin, permissive and accommodating to the culture. How one views the Scriptures reflects whether he or she is traveling the high road to restoration or the well-beaten path to apostasy.

• *First* is the challenge of substituting "performance worship" for the practice of worship in spirit and truth with the mind. Worship in the temple was a performance by a priest with flickering candles, sweet-smelling incense, the sound and smell of animal sacrifices and trained singers with instrumental music. It was very impressive. Christian worship is done by the individual himself and is an expression of praise and devotion to God. Worship is something you *do*, not something *done* to you. Its purpose is to express devotion to God, not impress men with performance.

• *Second* is the challenge of doing things that God "has not commanded." The Old Testament contains warnings about practicing unauthorized worship that God had not commanded (Leviticus 10:1-2; Deuteronomy 5:32; 18:20-21). Paul gave the same teachings in the New Testament: "And whatever you do in word or deed, do all in the name of the Lord" (Colossians 3:17).

• *Third* is the presumption on the part of some people that the silence of the Scriptures allows innovations. This challenge seeks to promote the idea that where the Scriptures are silent, one can do as he pleases. This false interpretation has led to the introduction of innovations of instrumental music, acceptance of unauthorized baptism, and leadership roles for women. If the restroom door says "Ladies," that excludes men and boys. If the Scriptures say "sing," that excludes everything not involved in singing. If the Scriptures say baptism is for the remission of sins, that excludes baptism as an outward sign of an inward grace.

• *Last* is the challenge of rejecting the authority of what is called "apostolic traditions" or "approved apostolic examples." The pattern of the apostolic church is not to be followed. That practice, according to this view, would make a person a "first-century Semite." The followers of this belief neglect to see that God's will has been taught not only in words but also by approved examples. What was exemplified in practice by apostolic authority should be regarded as scriptural authority.

APOSTOLIC TRADITIONS

The word "tradition" (*paradosis*) means that which has been "handed down" or "handed over." If it has been handed down by apostolic authority, it is binding. If it has been handed down by the traditions of men, it is not binding. The rejection of approved apostolic examples as authoritative is another one of the challenges facing the church.

Tradition is not always a bad word. Certainly if it binds something handed down by human traditions, it is wrong. Jesus condemned binding human traditions in the practice of true worship. Jesus confronted the Pharisees who tried to force human traditions on the apostles. He said: "And why do you yourselves transgress the commandment of God for the sake of your tradition? ... And thus you invalidated the word of God for the sake of your tradition" (Matthew 15:3, 5).

Tradition is also used in a good sense in the Scriptures. It refers to that which has been received from God and handed down to the men who wrote the New Testament. These are "apostolic traditions." They were inspired teachings or acts and must be regarded as authoritative. Paul used a technical literary formula in his letter to show that these apostolic traditions were to be followed. They were received by Paul from the Lord and delivered to the church. One example of this formula is given to the church at Corinth. The observance of the Lord's Supper was affirmed by Paul with this literary formula of "received and delivered." Not only were inspired words received from God, but also inspired practices were to be followed. Paul wrote:

For I received from the Lord that which I also delivered to

you, that the Lord Jesus in the night in which He was betrayed took bread; and when He had given thanks, He broke it and said, "This is My body which is for you; do this in remembrance of Me" (1 Corinthians 11:23-24).

Paul made it clear to the Corinthians that what he received from the Lord was to be delivered to those who follow the Lord.

He wrote the same things to Christians at Thessalonica: "So then, brethren, stand firm and hold to the traditions which you were taught, whether by word of mouth or by letter from us" (2 Thessalonians 2:15).

These passages show that what the apostles spoke, wrote and handed down by an approved apostolic example is to be followed. Noah followed the instructions on how to build the ark according to the pattern God gave to him. Moses was instructed to build the tabernacle "according to the pattern which was shown [him] on the mountain" (Exodus 25:40 NKJV).

Not all apostolic examples are to be followed. They must be approved apostolic examples. That is, the text and the context must show that the practice or doctrine was approved by apostolic authority and practiced by the church.

Christians need not meet in an upper room of a house located at Troas to observe the Lord's Supper because that is what Paul did (Acts 20:7-8). Where they met to observe the Lord's Supper was incidental to the command to observe the Lord's Supper. Observing the Lord's Supper on the first day of the week is an example of a practice of the apostolic church: "And on the first day of the week, when we were gathered together to break bread, Paul began talking to them" (v. 7).

Paul recognized that the church at Corinth gathered on the first day of every week and exhorted them to "put aside and save" when they came together (1 Corinthians 16:2). Coming together on the first day of the week is an approved apostolic example in which a collection was taken up.

The way the collection was to be taken up is not given. It could be done by passing around a basket, putting a box in the foyer, or any other way that would be orderly. How it is done is not revealed.

The silence of the Scripture is prohibitive in bringing into the work or worship of the church an innovation that God did not command and for which no Scriptural authority exists. The silence of the Scripture is permissive, however, concerning how to carry out a practice that is authorized.

FOR DISCUSSION

1. What are some ways false teachers seem to be affirming Scripture while actually denying its authority?

2. Why does religious compromise lead to apathy?

3. How does the Bible make people uncomfortable? What steps do they take to make its message more palatable?

4. How is emotionalism incompatible with biblical faith?

5. How is "performance worship" corrupting the church?

CHAPTER 7

THE TRANSMISSION OF THE SCRIPTURES

Ｈow can one believe in the inspiration and authority of the Scriptures when they are so far removed in time and culture from today's world? What relevance do old manuscripts from the distant past, written by diverse people in a primitive culture, have in the modern world? How can one accept these manuscripts as accurate in their transmission after they have been copied and recopied so many times? How can one even trust the text composed by men who had no idea of contemporary scientific theories, geographical knowledge or literary and historical criticism? How can we trust the selection of the canon done by the judgment of men? Is it naive still to believe in the promise of Jesus, "Heaven and earth will pass away, but My words shall not pass away" (Matthew 24:35)? This chapter will examine the trustworthiness of the Scriptures as they have come down to us.

Just as Jesus was both divine and human, the Scriptures are a divine message clothed in human words. In no way does this take away from their inspiration and authority. Just as the incarnation was a mystery beyond the understanding of man, so the inspiration of the Scriptures is a mystery beyond the understanding of man. Faith in the inspiration and authority of the Scriptures is an apriori decision of the will, a presupposition grounded in a faith that comes from hearing the Word of God. This presupposition does not mean no hard evidence exists for the inspiration of the Scriptures. This evidence has already been shown in Chapter 6.

This does not mean that a person blindly accepts every text from a manuscript or every judgment a translator gives to the meaning of the Hebrew or Greek words. Certainly it does not mean that every ancient manuscript is without errors or that any modern translation is totally accurate.

Avon Malone, in *The View of Inspiration as Reflected in Select Passages from the Pauline Epistles,* gave this balanced view of inspiration as portrayed in the writing of Paul:

> Paul's view of inspiration is one which sees every Scripture as "God-breathed" in such a way that the words, though drawn from the style and background of human writers, are words of the Holy Spirit. While making use of the writer's training and temperament, the Spirit exercises superintendence over the language employed so that the results, like the Incarnate Word, are both human and Divine (2).

Kippy Myers, in *Redeeming the Times*, gives this description of the divine and human aspects of the inspiration of Scriptures: "God controlled the process in such a way that he allowed the writers to draw from their backgrounds and vocabularies, while revealing the information and providing the guidance necessary to ensure a perfect product just as he intended" (11).

TEXTUAL CRITICISM

The science of textual criticism and the study of word meanings are important in discovering the original text and meaning of the words within the text. It is not the purpose of this chapter to accumulate evidence for inspiration or to give a history of textual criticism or critically study the oldest and best ancient manuscripts. These tasks have been done by others. Scholars in these fields have discovered and studied ancient manuscripts, divided them into textual families, discovered additions and omissions made by the copiers of the text, and critically compared the different texts in order to arrive at the most ancient and best readings.

They have sought to arrive as closely as possible to the original text.

There are thousands of ancient manuscripts of the Scriptures. One papyrus fragment containing parts of John 18 dates back to the early part of the second century. Three vellum, uncial manuscripts containing most of the New Testament date back to the fourth century. Although some textual variants can be found among them, the overwhelming content of their message is the same.

The Dead Sea Scrolls, preserved in well-sealed jars, were discovered in 1947 in caves not far from the Dead Sea. These scrolls contain portions of almost all the books in the Old Testament as well as a number of manuscripts thought to belong to the Essene party of the Jews. Most of these manuscripts are thought to be dated somewhere between the first century B.C. and the first century A.D. They are several hundred years older than any manuscript of the Old Testament known at the time of their discovery. When these manuscripts were compared to the Masoretic text (the Old Testament in Hebrew), and the Septuagint (the Old Testament in Greek), no significant differences were found. This discovery helped to confirm the accuracy of our contemporary text.

Textual critics are sometimes uncertain about which ancient text to follow when minor variants occur in the different manuscripts.

An example of this is found in the confession made by the Ethiopian eunuch before he was baptized. The eunuch asked Philip, "What prevents me from being baptized?" (Acts 8:36). Philip responded: " 'If you believe with all your heart, you may.' And he answered and said, 'I believe that Jesus Christ is the Son of God' " (v. 37).

This passage is in the Western Text family but absent from some of the oldest and most complete manuscripts. It was quoted by some of the earliest church fathers and its teaching is confirmed by other Scripture. No doctrine or practice rests on this passage alone. The King James Version retained it, but the American Standard Version and most of the other modern versions place it in footnotes. It has a good textual background, but for some reason it was not included in some of the major early manuscripts.

Another textual problem surrounds the ending of Mark's Gospel. Three different endings are found in the ancient manuscripts. Some manuscripts have a shorter ending after Mark 16:8. Other manuscripts stop at Mark 16:8. The longest and best-attested ending, Mark 16:9-20, is found in most translations. The New American Standard has the long ending in the text, and the shorter ending in the margin. No doctrine or practice rests on this text alone. It, too, is quoted by some of the earliest church fathers.

The transcription of the text was done under difficult circumstances in ancient times. No photocopying machines or printing presses were available. Copies were made by a scribe who dipped his quill in ink and then marked one letter at a time on a vellum or parchment scroll. Spell checks, editors or proofreaders were not available. Human error can be seen in the work.

A comparison of the multitude of manuscripts that have been preserved from the different text families can provide a basis for discovering with confidence the message of the original text.

More copies of the Scriptures have been preserved than any other ancient writing. The Scriptures have been translated into more languages than any other body of literature. The science of textual criticism that has been developed is able to detect scribal errors, missing words, and additions to the original text. The meaning of words in a text can be understood because of the science of etymology. One can determine the origin of a word, its development and its meaning at different times and in different localities.

Not all textual problems have been resolved. Not all word meanings are clear. There is room for continued study. Certainly there is the promise of Jesus that His Word would not pass away (Matthew 24:35). This promise is not fulfilled by a miracle, but by understanding and following the laws of logic and using the tools of science.

THE CANON

The word "canon" means "a rule or a standard." When referring to the Scriptures, canon means the standard by which a document might be considered a part of the inspired and authoritative Scriptures. God did not provide us a list of the Old Testament or New Testament books dropped down from heaven. The Holy Spirit gives no sign from heaven to confirm the books of the canon. Like the incarnation, both divine and human sides must be considered.

The promise and the providence of God are on the divine side. Jesus promised that His words would never pass away. He said, "Heaven and earth shall pass away, but My words shall not pass away" (Matthew 24:35). God spoke the universe into existence by His word at the beginning and sustains creation by His word even now. He will destroy the world by His word at the end of time and ultimately judge all of mankind by His word. He revealed His will for man through His word in Scriptures.

Providence as used here refers to God's behind-the-scene workings in the world by His laws to accomplish His will. When God overruled His laws spoken into existence at the creation of the world, the result is considered a miracle. Jesus raised the dead, walked on water, and made the blind to see. These were miracles.

When God works in history according to His laws to accomplish His will, it is providence. God has worked in both ways. The giving of His Word to holy men of God who were moved by the Holy Spirit was a miracle. The preservation of that word in time and history is providential.

God has worked in history in a providential way to formulate the canon as we now have it today. The Holy Spirit inspired oral sermons, apostles' letters, and other writings at the time they were spoken or written. The choice and collection of these documents is also the work of God done through the providential working of God using the human process of critical thinking and a reasonable faith.

Critical thinking was used in the process of canonizing the books of the Bible. Several criteria were used. First, the writing had to be of apostolic origin. Second, it was to be in conformity to other Scriptures. Third, it was to have been traditionally accepted by apostolic churches. Fourth, it must be useful in refuting false religions and error. All of these factors were brought together to determine what is to be regarded as Scripture.

The formation of the canon began in the apostolic age. The early church had the Old Testament Scriptures, and they were considered to be inspired and authoritative. The church added to this body of Scriptures the writings of the apostles and other inspired prophets to make the New Testament Scriptures. Some of the writers of the New Testament Scriptures quoted as Scriptures material found within the New Testament itself. The New Testament writers were already regarding certain sayings and writings as Scripture.

• *First,* Peter recognized the writings of Paul as being on the same level as Scriptures:

> [A]nd regard the patience of our Lord to be salvation; just as also our beloved brother Paul, according to the wisdom given him, wrote to you, as also in all his letters, speaking in them of those things, in which are some things hard to understand, which the untaught and unstable distort, as they do also the rest of the Scriptures (2 Peter 3:15-16).

• *Second,* the sayings of Jesus are regarded as Scripture by Paul. One of the proverbs Jesus gave to the apostles in the limited commission was: "[T]he laborer is worthy of his wages" (Luke 10:7; Matthew 10:10). Paul quoted this saying in 1 Timothy 5:18 and introduced it by the formula, "For the Scripture says." This passage is not found in the Old Testament, but Paul quoted it as Scripture. He regarded the sayings of Jesus to be the Word of God.

• *Third,* the letters Paul wrote claimed that they possessed the authority of God. The instructions Paul gave to the church concerning the Lord's Supper were from the Lord Himself. He wrote, "For I received from the Lord that which I also delivered to you" (1 Corinthians 11:23). The same letter contains instructions concerning the role of women in the church. The authority of these instructions came not only from the custom of the churches, the Law, and his own apostolic authority; they were from the Lord Himself: "If anyone thinks he is a prophet or spiritual, let him recognize that the things that I write to you are the Lord's commandment" (1 Corinthians 14:37).

The Scriptures were regarded as inspired and authoritative from the time of their composition. The formal formation of the canon as a religious authority arose from the need to reject heretics. Many pseudepigraphous gospels and letters written by false teachers claimed to be from an apostle. A standard was developed by which the church could separate the genuine writings from the counterfeit. The books now contained in the New Testament came to be accepted generally even during the apostolic age. Some books were questioned in some places because they were not known in all of the churches, but time and communication solved this problem. Some were rejected because they were false documents imitating the accepted book and used by false teachers to support their false doctrines. The books of the New Testament were eventually universally confirmed. They have been tried and tested by time, use and critical thinking. They were regarded as inspired and authoritative in the apostolic age and have stood the tests of time, truthfulness and the questioning of men.

By the end of the second century most of the 27 New Testament books in our canon were firmly established. They were quoted by such apostolic fathers as Papias, Polycarp, Justin Martyr, Irenaeus and Clement of Rome. At the beginning of the third century, both Origen and Clement of Alexandria quoted from the 27 books of the established canon. The Council of Carthage in A.D. 397 listed all 27 books as being apostolic and a part of the canon. The judgment of the Council did not make them inspired and authoritative but only gave the accumulated judgment of most of the churches.

TRANSLATIONS

The rapid growth and spread of the early church through persecution brought about a need for translations from the Greek Scriptures into other languages.

In A.D. 160, Tatian produced a harmony of the four gospels in Syriac called the diatessaron. The Old Latin version was made before the end of the second century, and a Coptic version was known around the beginning of the third century. Other versions in various languages quickly came upon the scene. Since that time, the translations have multiplied until only a few dialects do not have at least a portion of the Scriptures in their own language.

Problems can be found in the hand copying of the ancient biblical text. Human errors are to be found even in the best manuscripts. Problems are also in the translating of Greek words into another language. Sometimes no word fully translates the meaning of the Greek term. Shades of meaning cannot be conveyed from one language into another language. An example is that the Greek language has four words translated by the English word "love." Shades of the meaning in this Greek word are difficult to translate into English. The Greek term *"storge"* carries the meaning of family love. The Greek term *"phileo"* carries with it the meaning of friendship love. The Greek term *"agapao"* carries with it the meaning of a willed love.

In seeking the meaning of a passage of Scriptures, one should seek both the best Greek text produced through the strict guidelines of textual criticism and the most literal and understandable English translation. Sometimes the most literal is not the most understandable. Sometimes the most understandable is not the most literal. This problem can be overcome by comparing a literal translation with a translation that is easy to understand.

An example can be found in the American Standard Version (ASV) and the New International Version (NIV). The American Standard is one of the most literal. The New International Version is one of the most readable. By comparing the two versions one can perhaps come to the best understanding of the text. The English Standard Bible (ESV), introduced in 2001, seeks to give both accuracy and understanding.

A good Bible dictionary is helpful in understanding words in a translation that are obsolete, technical or unclear. A concordance is also helpful in seeing how the word might be used in other contexts. A critical commentary can also add to the understanding of the text.

THE BEST TRANSLATION

The best translation of the Scriptures is to be found in the life of a believer. A person will be more apt to believe in Christ when he sees a change in the way a person acts, speaks and lives when he becomes a Christian. This is emphasized throughout the New Testament:

> Let your light shine before men in such a way that they may see your good works, and glorify your Father who is in heaven (Matthew 5:16).

> Do all things without grumbling or disputing; that you may prove yourselves to be blameless and innocent, children of God above reproach in the midst of a crooked and perverse generation, among whom you appear as lights in the world (Philippians 2:14-16).

The Word of God, the Scriptures, is inspired. Men were guided by the Holy Spirit in their writing so that even when their vocabulary was from their native tongue and their cultural background was from diverse regions, what they spoke and wrote was from the Holy Spirit. They were able to speak the Word of God clearly and without error. They spoke and wrote as they were guided by the Holy Spirit

The transmission of the Scriptures, however, is from man and is subject to all of the weaknesses of men. Men made mistakes in copying the text, perhaps adding or omitting a word or phrase. Such mistakes can be found and corrected through the science of textual criticism. Words change in their meaning through time and culture, but this can be overcome through the study of the words used in the thousands of preserved ancient manuscripts. Lexicons and dictionaries are excellent tools to use in getting back to the original meaning of a word or phrase.

We have the help of trained scholars who by textual criticism can arrive at the best and most ancient text. We have the help of trained linguists who are able to discover the shades of meaning that a word might have in one language and can best translate it into another dialect. This is the human part of the Scriptures. Trusting the integrity and common sense of the scholars and the providence of God, one can know the Scriptures are inspired and authoritative in all areas in which they speak. They are the source of all religious authority. This knowledge motivates a Bible believer to be "diligent to present [himself] approved to God as a workman who does not need to be ashamed, handling accurately the word of truth" (2 Timothy 2:15). The Scriptures came from God through the pens of men guided by the Holy Spirit. These writings are true, absolute, objective and understandable.

FOR DISCUSSION

1. How can we have confidence that the text of the Bible we use today is what was originally written?

2. How is questioning the accuracy of a particular manuscript different from doubting the authority of the Bible?

3. Are translations into modern languages inspired by God?

4. What version of the Bible do you use most and why?

CHAPTER 8

SCRIPTURE INTERPRETATION

A definitive passage on the interpretation of Scripture is found in Paul's admonition to Timothy who was told in the context of the growing apostasy in the church at Ephesus: "Be diligent to present yourself approved to God as a workman who does not need to be ashamed, handling accurately the word of truth" (2 Timothy 2:15).

Second Timothy is Paul's last letter to Timothy, his son in the gospel. The context of this passage shows that Timothy should avoid worldly and empty chatter and not participate in useless wrangling about words (2 Timothy 2:14-16). The false teachings of Hymenaeus and Philetus had infected the church at Ephesus like gangrene, destroying the faith of some. It was crisis time. The prediction Paul had made in his first letter was coming to pass. Some had fallen away (*apostesontai*) from the faith by "paying attention to deceitful spirits and doctrines of demons" (1 Timothy 4:1).

The remedy was to be found in "handling accurately the word of truth." This admonition included accepting it as inspired of God and interpreting it honestly.

The technical word for interpretation, "hermeneutics," is derived from the Greek term "*diermeneuo*." In the Greek pantheon, Hermes was the messenger and interpreter of Jupiter. Hermeneutics is the process of delivering the word of truth and interpreting it so that it can be understood. The term as used in this book is the science of interpreting the Scripture.

A form of the word *"diermeneuo"* can be found in Luke's account of Jesus' conversation with the two men from Emmaus. The text says that Jesus "beginning with Moses ... explained [*diermeneusev*] to them the things concerning Himself in all the Scriptures" (Luke 24:27).

Scripture interpretation was involved in the conversion of the eunuch. "Philip opened his mouth, and beginning from this Scripture, he preached Jesus to him" (Acts 8:35). By hermeneutics, he showed how the predictions of Isaiah 53 referred to Jesus.

If one can handle the word of truth the right way, he can also handle it the wrong way. Jesus condemned the Jews because they were handling the Scriptures the wrong way. He said, "You search the Scriptures, because you think that in them you have eternal life; and it is these that bear witness of Me" (John 5:39).

Peter warned that the "untaught and unstable" would distort the Scriptures (2 Peter 3:16). Even the devil distorted the Scriptures when he tempted Jesus (Matthew 4:6).

PRESUPPOSITIONS

An inspired set of rules by which the Scriptures can be interpreted does not exist. Like the preservation and translation of the text, interpretation depends on the critical and consistent judgment of men.

The way a passage is interpreted reveals one's presuppositions on how he regards the Scriptures. No man lives in a vacuum. One cannot come to the Scriptures without presuppositions and prejudice. Readers need to use reason in interpreting the Scriptures. Consistency, logic and integrity are important. An honest heart and a secure ego will acknowledge this. Those who question the inspiration, authority and canon of the Scriptures need not bother with hermeneutics until they decide what they need to interpret and why it is important.

A person must come to the interpretation of Scripture with at least four presuppositions. These are not meant to be a complete list but will illustrate the importance of beginning at the beginning. One's presuppositions concerning the Scriptures need to be acknowledged before he begins the rational exercises of grammar, history, word meanings and context.

• **Presupposition #1:** God is a God of order. Science is possible because of His consistency with the laws of nature. A seed is planted, and it grows into a plant. The laws of nature demand that it must have water and sunshine; the laws of nature cause it to produce seed after its kind. Both reason and experience support this presupposition. God, who spoke the *kosmos* (orderly world) into existence out of nothing, surely must be orderly and consistent in all that He does. Plants and animals reproduce after their kind. Planets stay in their orbits, and seas stay within their bounds. All has been decreed by the God of order and consistency. We depend on this consistent order in using the scientific method for problem solving and plotting a course to Mars. It is impossible for God to contradict Himself (Hebrew 6:18).

The stars above us, nature around us, and the laws that govern all things demonstrate that God is a God of order.

• **Presupposition #2:** God reveals Himself in Scripture. This presupposition is grounded in a faith – a faith that is reasonable. The Word of God is the source of faith. Both reason and experience support this presupposition. If there is a creation, it is reasonable to presuppose that there is a Creator. The message of the Scriptures answers the many basic questions of existence asked by man. Where did man come from? What is good, and what is bad? Is there an afterlife? How can one erase the penalty of sin? What is God like? The Scriptures give the only consistent and satisfying answers to such questions. Rejecting the knowledge of God results in worshiping idols and, finally, in gross immoral conduct. Of this progress into apostasy by the pagan world, Paul says,

> For even though they knew God, they did not honor Him as God, or give thanks; but they became futile in their speculations, and their foolish heart was darkened. Professing to be wise, they became fools, and exchanged the glory of the incorruptible God for an image in the form of corruptible man and of birds and four-footed animals and crawling creatures (Romans 1:21-23).

• **PRESUPPOSITION #3:** The Scriptures are absolute, true and complete. Archaeology, ancient historical writings and fulfilled predictions support this affirmation. The Scriptures themselves make claim to being true, absolute and complete. Jesus said His Word is eternal. It would not pass away (Matthew 24:35). His Word is true (John 17:17). Men have tried to discount the Bible by claiming that it does not agree with the facts of science, history, geography, the origins of matter and the spirit of man.

Again, the passing of time has confirmed that what Robert Ingersoll termed as the "mistakes of Moses" were really the mistakes of Ingersoll. His once popular book, *Some Mistakes of Moses*, can hardly be found today, but the Scriptures, which tell of the life and work of Moses, are more broadly distributed than any other book ever printed.

• **PRESUPPOSITION #4:** The Scriptures are consistent, understandable and true. One need not prove it because its message fits the needs of diverse people with different backgrounds. Both reason and experience support this presupposition. The Scriptures claim such for themselves. Jesus quoted the Scriptures to His enemies and added the "Scripture cannot be broken" (John 10:35). The writer of Hebrews said, "It is impossible for God to lie" (Hebrews 6:18).

One comes to doubt the truthfulness of the Scriptures, not because they contradict truth, but because they do not fit what he wants to believe. Jesus said, "If any man is willing to do His will, he shall know of the teaching, whether it is of God, or whether I speak from Myself" (John 7:17).

When one has a problem with the inspiration and authority of the Scriptures, it is not because they can be shown to be false. His problem is with the presupposition of faith. When one has a problem believing and understanding the Scriptures, it is not because the message is untrue; it may be that his heart is deceived or hardened.

METHODS OF INTERPRETATION

Hermeneutics has a long and varied history. This method of interpretation dates at least to the Greek philosopher, Democritus, in the fifth century B.C. and probably was practiced even earlier. The Greek philosophers used the hermeneutical tool of allegory to interpret the classical poets of Greece.

Rabbinic hermeneutics is also very ancient, dating to the time of Ezra's return from Babylonian captivity. The returning Jews did not understand the law or the language in which the law was written. Nehemiah recorded how Ezra had the law read and interpreted to the assembled people: "[The readers] explained the law to the people while the people remained in their place. And they read from the book, from the law of God, translating to give the sense so that they understood the reading" (Nehemiah 8:7-8).

The scribes and the Pharisees considered themselves interpreters of the law, but many whom Jesus confronted were manipulators of the law. A second century A.D. Jewish tract titled "The Sayings of the Fathers" reflects the idea that interpretations were handed down from generation to generation and thus became authoritative. The interpretations became more important than the law:

> Moses received the Torah from Sinai and delivered it to Joshua, and Joshua to the elders, and the elders to the prophets, and the prophets delivered it to the men of the Great Synagogue. They said three things: Be deliberate in judgment, raise up many disciples and make a fence around the Torah (Blackman 66).

The problem was that the scribes and Pharisees made their interpretations the religious standard rather than the Torah. They became adept at twisting the Scriptures to justify what they wanted to believe and do. They built a fence of interpretation around the law until the law was nullified. Matthew recorded such an incident. Jesus was asked "Why do Your disciples transgress the tradition of the elders? ... [Jesus answered], And why do you yourselves transgress the commandment of God for the sake of your tradition?" (Matthew 15:2-3).

Interpretations can be good or bad. They can reveal the meaning of Scriptures that are difficult to understand, as in Ezra's case. Such interpretations are good if they are done honestly and critically. But they also can conceal the meaning of the Scriptures if, like the scribes and Pharisees, one interprets them to justify what he wants to do. This kind of faulty interpretation still exists today. The Scriptural teaching is ignored, and the interpretation becomes religious authority.

Allegorical interpretations were applied to the Greek translation of the Old Testament Scriptures called the Septuagint. When Philo of Alexandria, a contemporary of Jesus, sought to relate the Septuagint to Greek philosophy, something had to give. Because Philo could not make them fit together consistently, he allegorized. If the Scriptures contained something he could not explain or which seemed unworthy of God, he refused to take the literal meaning. For him there were two levels in every passage of Scripture, the literal and the spiritual. He clearly regarded the spiritual to be the superior level. Following the tradition of Philo and continuing past the time of Origin, hermeneutics in Alexandria took the road of allegory.

A rival school of thought was to be found in Antioch of Syria. Under the influence of Theodore and Chrysostom, this school rejected allegorical interpretation. They understood the Scriptures literally and within the historical setting in which they were written. They used a more critical method of interpretation, employing sound grammatical and historical data as well as common sense. They studied the text within its context, refusing ecclesiastical traditions and allegories as a basis for their interpretation.

Medieval hermeneutics tended to ignore the original and literal sense of the Scriptures. There was a universal ignorance of the Hebrew and Greek languages. Most people and many priests could not even read and write. A few attempts were made to employ hermeneutics, such as making the text more understandable by placing notes in the margin of the manuscripts, a method called *glossa ordinari*. More often, the text was ignored in deference to propositional speculations of theology. Scholasticism prevailed.

Hermeneutics during the Reformation period had a rebirth. An attempt was made to return to the Scriptures and to reason. The Scriptures were no longer isolated in the monasteries and read only by the priests. Biblical languages were studied. Translations were made and given to the people in a language they understood. Roland H. Bainton, in his book *Here I Stand, A Life of Martin Luther*, quotes Luther's reputed statement at his trial at Worms as reflecting some of the signs of the time:

Unless I am convinced by the testimony of the Scriptures or by clear reason, (for I do not trust either in the pope or in councils alone, since it is well known that they have often erred and contradicted themselves), I am bound by the Scriptures I have quoted and my conscience is captive to the Word of God. I cannot and I will not retract anything, since it is neither safe nor right to go against conscience. God help me. Amen. Here I stand, I cannot do otherwise (Luther's Works, 32:103-31) (81).

The important question began to be, "What do the Scriptures say?" more than "What is the ecclesiastical dogma?" The Bible began to be regarded more as the central and supreme authority in religion. The idea of going back to the Bible and restoring New Testament Christianity became widespread in Europe. Leaders like Martin Luther, John Calvin and Ulrich Zwingli arose resisting the Roman Catholic doctrine and practices without biblical authority. Other groups called "Anabaptists" were more thorough in their reforms. Together these groups in time were called the Protestant Reformation.

What began in several places as a noble ideal disintegrated into a confused conglomeration of denominations dominated by personalities, parties and politics. Some ignored certain scriptural practices and others substituted religious teachings and practices from both past and contemporary cultures. The results ended in a partial reform of medieval Roman Catholicism rather than a restoration of New Testament Christianity.

FOR DISCUSSION

1. What dangers arise when the Bible is not handled accurately?

2. What is required of a Bible student if he or she is going to interpret Scripture correctly?

3. Why was biblical interpretation important in the Reformation Movement of the 16th century?

4. Why are allegorical interpretations of Scripture popular among many religious groups?

CHAPTER 9

METHODS OF INTERPRETATION

In the third century, Tertullian asked, "What has Athens to do with Jerusalem, the academy with the church?" He was the first of a long line of individuals who thought there was a conflict between faith and reason, between the scholar and the saint. This battle continues. On one side is the pseudo-intellectual with a scholarly disdain for faith. On the other side is the irrational religionist with a stubborn prejudice against reason.

Faith and reason are not enemies. Faith is based upon the declarations of God in the Scriptures at different times and in different places. Reason is based upon the consistency of nature's laws that God spoke into existence at the beginning. Faith and reason are not alien to one another. Both are true and consistent. Each complements the other when properly understood.

Anselm and Aquinas, medieval theologians, tried to prove the existence of God by reason. Like Aristotle and Plato, they could reason back to the logical necessity of the "first cause," but they could not come close to proving the God of the Bible by rational deduction. The Bible is the inspired Word of God. It reveals the "first cause" sought by philosophers. Its truthfulness is accepted by faith, and reason supports this faith. Its teachings are reasonable and consistent.

The way that reason fits into the affirmation of faith strengthens faith. True faith is reasonable.

Only through an exercise of reason can one understand revelation. Language can be understood only by reason. Truth is believed only by the reasoning process. Error can be exposed only by reason. Right and wrong, good and bad, truth and error can be determined only when reason and revelation are brought together.

A large part of the contemporary culture rejects the idea of absolute, objective truth. Truth for them is relative and cannot be communicated by language. Such an idea is a contradiction within itself. Is one not stating what he believes to be an absolute truth when he says, "There is no absolute truth"? If truth is relative, so is this statement.

Without divine revelation, everyone would do what is right in his or her own eyes. Without reasonable hermeneutics to understand this divine revelation, everyone would believe what he or she wants to believe. Some processes of understanding Scriptures that pose as hermeneutics are unreasonable and erroneous.

Experiential hermeneutics is contrary to reason. Interpretations using this kind of hermeneutics are as diverse as the individuals who claim the experience. If these diverse interpretations are from God, then truth is relative, and God contradicts Himself. Expressions from those who hold to this kind of hermeneutics include: "I know it is true because I feel it down in my heart"; "What does this passage mean "to you?"; "I don't care what the Bible says, I know that God knows my heart."

Traditional hermeneutics is that which has been handed down from the past or handed over from the present. In Roman Catholicism, it is the voice of the church. In Protestantism, it is the statements of the creeds. Sometimes it is merely what some esteemed brother has said or some practice that has been sanctified by time.

Polemic hermeneutics begins with a doctrine one wants to believe or a ritual one wants to practice followed by an interpretation of the Scriptures in a way that will allow it. How amazing to see the creativity of men when they are thus motivated! Using this type of hermeneutics, one can find infant baptism in the conversion of the household of Cornelius. One can find the pope in a play on the Greek word "*petros*" in Matthew 16:18. One can find instrumental music in the Greek word "*psallo*" by referring to its meaning in the classical period 500 years before its use in the New Testament and ignoring its use in the *koine* period. He can deny baptism as being necessary to salvation by rejecting the ending of Mark and ignoring other passages that teach the same thing.

Using hermeneutics in an effort to prove what one already believes too often leads to compromise. Perhaps it is better to say that compromise too often leads to faulty hermeneutics.

One can accept by faith the inspiration and authority of the Scriptures based on an act of the will, hearing the Word of God, and the support of logical evidence. One can accept by faith the text and canon of the Scriptures by an act of the will, the promise of Jesus, and a multitude of supportive evidence from the critical examination of ancient manuscripts. One can accept the Scriptures by faith as an act of the will. Understanding them comes by critical study. The same process might be used to understand any written communication. The meaning of the words, the structure of the sentences, the rules of grammar, the context in which they were written are all important. Reason must be used.

RULES OF INTERPRETATION

Alexander Campbell understood the importance of reason in understanding the Scriptures. In his book, *The Christian System*, he outlined seven rules to follow in seeking to find the meaning of Scriptures. They were the guidelines of his hermeneutics. They combined faith in the Scriptures and reason to understand the Word of God. In an abbreviated form these rules are:

1. In studying any of the Scriptures, one must consider the historical circumstances of the book. These are the order, the title, the author, the date, the place and the occasion of it.
2. One must observe who speaks and under what dispensation he officiates. Consider the persons addressed, their prejudices, character and religious relations.
3. To understand the meaning of a text, the same philological principles, deduced from the nature of language, or the same laws of interpretation that are applied to the language of other books must be respected.

4. Common usage, which can only be ascertained by testimony, must always decide the meaning of any word that has but one signification; but when words have, according to testimony, more meanings than one, whether literal or figurative, the scope, the context or parallel passages must decide the meaning.

5. In all figurative language, ascertain the point of resemblance and judge the nature of the trope and its kind from the point of resemblance.

6. In the interpretation of symbols, types, allegories and parables, this rule is supreme. One must ascertain the point to be illustrated because comparison is never to be extended beyond that point.

7. For the salutary and sanctifying intelligence of the Oracles of God, the following rule is indispensable: one must come within the understanding distance.

Campbell further adds this statement about the importance of the attitude of the reader: "Every one, then, who opens the Book of God, with one aim, with one ardent desire – intent only to know the will of God – to such a person the knowledge of God is easy; for the Bible is framed to illuminate such, and only such, with salutary knowledge of things celestial and divine" (2-5).

Campbell sought to bring to the understanding of the Scriptures both faith and reason. They mingle. Without faith, the Scriptures become merely an ancient writing of curiosity. Without reason, understanding the Scriptures becomes impossible. By faith, we accept the Scriptures as inspired, and by reason we are able to understand their message.

Faith and reason are essential in understanding the will of God. Reason is used to discover why two passages may seem contradictory. Reason is used to see if one's understanding of the text is correct or if the context is understood. One uses reason to discover the best text from a multitude of ancient manuscripts that are available. Reason is used to determine in what age the passage was spoken and to whom the passage is addressed. But by faith the reader comes to regard the Scriptures as God's Word.

RESTORATION HERMENEUTICS

The renewed study of hermeneutics has resulted in what some call "restoration hermeneutics." This hermeneutical method some suggest refers to the kind of hermeneutics traditionally used by leaders in the American Restoration Movement. Such was the product of the age that the American Restoration Movement began and is not necessarily relevant to the culture today.

In two articles in the *Restoration Quarterly* in 1989, Michael Casey gave a history of these hermeneutical principles and the historical stream of thought that influenced the early leaders of the Restoration Movement. He suggested that the accepted methods of interpretation in the American Restoration Movement were command, example and necessary inference. The background of restoration hermeneutics, however, was from many streams of thought.

The Italian Renaissance viewed the highest ideal to be a return to the past – Greek and Roman cultures. This influenced the thinking of such leaders as Luther, Calvin and Zwingli, who rejected ecclesiastical traditions of the Roman Catholic church. They looked back to the ideal pattern of the New Testament church and sought to return to the Scriptures.

The English influence, through the Puritans and the Westminster Confession, reflected many restoration ideals. The philosophical influence of Sir Francis Bacon, the Scottish Common Sense Realists, and the writings of John Locke influenced certain leaders of the American Restoration Movement. One cannot question that this kind of philosophical climate influenced the new American culture including the leaders of the Restoration Movement.

A new spirit was permeating the new nation. Political freedom, new frontiers, as well as freedom from religious bondage provided a climate for the rejection of old ecclesiastical domination and a desire to renew a scriptural affirmation of faith and practice. One must be aware of such influences upon the leaders of the early American Restoration Movement. They did not live in a vacuum. Many were rejecting the Roman Catholic traditions and the Protestant creeds. It was an age that emphasized critical thinking. Truth was to be discovered through a rational and logical process. The United States was a new nation with new thinking. Common sense, rather than ecclesiastical dogma, seemed the natural course be used in understanding the Scriptures.

One doubts, however, that such a settled standard of Scripture interpretation existed among leaders of the American Restoration Movement. The leaders of the movement came from different religious backgrounds, different geographical areas, and different educational levels. Religious leaders of the movement differed in the way they interpreted the text. This fact is evident in the several groups that separated to form distinctive religious organizations.

Those who went into Mormonism viewed the Scriptures as incomplete and sought new revelation. They relied on an experiential authority from latter day prophets. They added other books that they considered inspired. Through the influence of Sidney Rigdon, an early preacher in the American Restoration Movement, a significant number of the Restoration churches went into Mormonism. *The Book of Mormon, The Pearl of Great Price* and *The Doctrine of the Covenant* were regarded by those who became Mormons as equal to the Old Testament and the New Testament. The Scriptures are viewed only as a part of God's revelation to man.

The major division of the American Restoration Movement came at the beginning of the 20th century over different views of the Scriptures. Those who evolved into the Disciples of Christ came to believe that the Scriptures were not authoritative in doctrine but must be compromised with the culture to attain unity. Their leaders generally had what came to be known as a low view of the inspiration of the Scriptures.

Those who evolved into the Independent Christian Church accepted the permissive silence of the Scripture that allowed anything not specifically condemned in the Scriptures. The Independent Christian Church broke with the Disciples because they were unwilling to accept some practices of the Disciples denomination. Today diverse practices exist among those in the Independent Christian Churches. Some are similar to the Disciples but unwilling to be considered a part of that denomination. Others are more like churches of Christ but want to retain the permissive silence of the Scriptures.

Leaders in the churches of Christ have historically resisted the pressures to become an ecumenical denomination, a human ecclesiastical organization, or to accept an open-ended hermeneutic to determine their faith and practice. They view the Scriptures as inspired and authoritative. They seek to be involved in a perpetual restoration of faith and practice of the apostolic church. The restoration principle is still alive and well. They hold to no creed, no central organization and no clergy. Nothing is involved in their faith and practice that cannot be supported by Scripture.

Recent events, however, show that some in churches of Christ are considering uniting with the Independent Christian Church. In 2004, speakers at one lectureship and a preacher in a large church in Texas advocated union with the Independent Christian Church. It remains to be seen how broad and influential this challenge will be. The outcome will be determined by how the Scriptures are viewed.

The Disciples church saw the American Restoration Movement as a unity movement to include all believers in Christ with little regard to their faith and practice. They sought to unite with denominations of every variety. They introduced instrumental music into their worship, accepted human organizations to do the work of the church, and rejected baptism as essential to salvation. They continue to seek unity with denominational churches and, according to one author, the Disciples church is the fastest declining religious group in the United States. This segment of the Restoration Movement walked the path of unity but not the path of restoration of the teaching and practice of the apostolic church. This led them to accept the use of instrumental music in worship, the practice of women spiritual leaders in the role of preachers and elders, and accommodations to and unity with denominational organizations.

There never had been, nor should there be, a closed, standardized hermeneutic or ecclesiastical creed. If this ever happens in the churches of Christ, they will cease to be a movement and become a denomination. Certainly differences exist among different groups. Some of the differences involve opinions and must not cause a break in fellowship. These differences need to be resolved by oral debates, written exchanges and personal discussions. A widespread conviction among the members of churches of Christ holds that an open mind, a believing heart and common sense can resolve these differences. Scripture interpretation is always a quest, never a "once for all" closed system.

Some have turned away from the church because they see her as only a product of a certain culture at a certain time in history. To them the church is no more than a human institution plagued with all the frailties and failures of men. Their view of the Scriptures is the basis for this view of the church.

No one is more negative toward the church or the Scriptures than a disillusioned believer. When one has lost faith in the Scriptures, the reasoning process that interprets them, and the church they reveal, he is doomed to live in a spiritual desert. He may pretend piety and accept a hermeneutic that can be used as a smoke screen to justify what he wants to believe and practice, but he will end up in apostasy.

FOR DISCUSSION

1. Why is reason an essential tool for a Christian to understand Scripture?

2. What are some sources of authority, other than Scripture, that people use to fashion their religion? What dangers do these pose for the church of Christ?

3. How does a change in biblical interpretation change the practices of the church? How do changes in church practice change the way people interpret the Bible?

4. Why has the low view of interpretation advanced by the community church movement led their leaders to seek closer fellowship with the Christian Church?

5. How does correct interpretation produce a biblical unity in the church?

CHAPTER 10

THE RESTORATION PRINCIPLE

How one views the Scriptures determines his religion. Just because one claims to accept Scripture does not mean he or she regards the Bible as the Word of God and, therefore, the standard for all religious faith and practice. Roman Catholics accept the Scriptures, but they provide an interpretation based on their traditions and the statements of the pope when he speaks ex cathedra. Protestants accept the Scriptures, but interpret them according to their creeds. Mormons accept the Scriptures, but they want to add what they consider to be latter-day revelations given in the Book of Mormon.

Many different religions claim to follow the Scriptures, but they differ widely in their faith and practice. The reason is that their views of Scripture are different.

The devil contradicted the Word of God when he tempted Adam and Eve in the Garden of Eden. God had said concerning the tree in the midst of the garden, "You shall not eat from it, or touch it, lest you die" (Genesis 3:3). The devil contradicted the Word of God and said, "You surely shall not die!" When what is done in religion is contrary to the Word of God, it is following the example of the devil.

When Jesus was tempted in the wilderness after fasting 40 days, the devil took Him up to the pinnacle of the temple and said to Him: "If You are the Son of God throw Yourself down; for it is written, 'He will give His angels charge concerning You'; and 'On their hands they will bear You up, Lest You strike Your foot against a stone' " (Matthew 4:6).

The devil took the Scripture out of context to tempt Jesus. He used what we call the permissive silence of the Scripture to tempt Jesus to worship Him. The Scripture did not state, "Thou shall not worship the devil." This was not needed. The Scripture said, "[Y]ou shall worship the Lord your God and serve Him." This text is from Deuteronomy 6:13, but Jesus added the word "only." He said, "You shall worship the Lord your God and serve Him only." The Scripture did not have to name all of the false gods one must not worship. It said that one should worship the true God, and that excluded all others.

We will discuss three things in this chapter. First, the restoration principle will be defined and shown to be a valid way of following the teachings of Jesus Christ. Second, the restoration principle will be shown to be biblical, reasonable and workable today. Third, churches of Christ are the consequence of applying the restoration principle in the 21st century.

The acceptance of the validity of the restoration principle reflects one's view of the Scripture. Chapter 3 affirmed the inspiration and authority of the Scriptures. If one accepts the Scriptures as inspired and authoritative, then the restoration principle will follow. The rejection of the restoration principle is really a faith problem.

Roy Bowen Ward stated in his speech at the 1965 Pepperdine Lectureship:

> If the restoration principle is defined as one which acknowledges the Christ event as unique and final, and one which accepts the inspired apostolic witness, vis., the canon of the New Testament, as the unique and final authority standard for the church until the Second Coming, then this restoration principle is valid. The principle is not only valid, but it necessarily inheres in Christianity. ...
>
> Churches of Christ owe their existence, historically speaking to the allegiance to this restoration principle. If the restoration principle is not valid, the existence of the churches of Christ then would appear – may I say – ridiculous (57-58).

The acceptance of the restoration principle is the basis for the very existence of churches of Christ. Churches of Christ have no reason for existence if the restoration principle is not valid. Those who claim identity with the church of Christ as reflected in the New Testament are living a contradiction if they reject the restoration principle.

Tragically, the restoration principle is being re-examined today. Some prominent preachers and professors have rejected it saying that it is impossible to restore the church and, even if it were possible, it would not be desirable because it would be out of touch with the times.

DEFINED

The idea of the restoration principle is described in the Scriptures themselves: "All Scripture is inspired by God and profitable for teaching, for reproof, for correction, for training in righteousness; that the man of God may be adequate, equipped for every good work" (2 Timothy 3:16-17.)

The Scriptures are an adequate standard of faith and practice for those who would follow Jesus Christ. The Scriptures contain the pattern or blueprint showing man how he may be adequately equipped to every good work. The word that is translated "correction" is "*epanorthosin*." The meaning given to this root word by Kittle and Friedrich in *Theological Dictionary of the New Testament* is "restoration, reform, re-establish and correction." The Scriptures are the basis for bringing the church back into her original state. It presupposes that the danger of apostasy, a falling away from the original model of the church established by Jesus, is ever present. Apostasies occur in every generation. There must also be a perpetual restoration in every generation.

Barton W. Stone, in the *Last Will and Testament of the Springfield Presbytery,* 200 years ago said, "We will, that the people henceforth take the Bible as the only sure guide to heaven."

Thomas Campbell in the "Declaration and Address" stated, "Our desire therefore, for ourselves and our brethren would be ... returning to and holding fast by the original standard; taking the Divine word alone for our rule." His objective was "to conform to the model; and adopt the practice of the ideal primitive church, expressly exhibited in the New Testament" (Murch 42-51).

The restoration of the New Testament church is not a restoration of the church at Corinth with all of its problems or the church at Ephesus which even in Paul's day contained the seeds of apostasy. One also should not confuse restoration as being a return to the church of the 1940s or even the 19th-century Restoration Movement. Restoration means a restoration of the ideal church as portrayed in the New Testament. The restoration principle is the acceptance of the pattern and faith of the ideal church of Christ reflected in the New Testament as being the pattern and faith of the church of Christ in the 21st century. It is a call of "back to the Bible" as a standard of faith and practice.

The last 40 years have seen a restudy of the restoration principle. This process is healthy. One must not accept uncritically anything handed down from the past. If the restoration principle cannot stand the searchlight of truth and the exposure of investigation, it should be rejected. If the restoration principle does not find its basis in the Scripture, it is unworthy. One should neither accept nor reject the restoration principle because it is old. Something does not have to be old to be true. Neither does it have to be true because it is new.

REJECTION OF THE RESTORATION PRINCIPLE

This restoration principle has been rejected by some in recent years because of three beliefs.

• *First,* it is rejected because one no longer views the Scripture as inspired and authoritative. A.T. DeGroot wrote in his book, *The Disciples of Christ, A History*: "Historical research cannot hope to discover and describe a church so primitive that it can be taken as an exact transcription of the mind of God in regard to what the church should be" (21).

• *Second,* the restoration principle is rejected because it is a hindrance to unity among believers. It has often been observed that the liberals in the American Restoration Movement emphasized unity among all believers, and the conservatives emphasized restoration of New Testament Christianity. Neither should be ignored. No real unity can occur unless it fits the pattern of the New Testament church. No restoration takes place until all of God's children are united in the body of Christ.

• *Third,* a basic reason, currently popular among many, is that the restoration principle is rejected because of a flawed hermeneutic. This comes from many sources. Again, quoting from Stendahl in his book

The Role of Women: "If something is a certain way in the New Testament, does that constitute the basic blueprint for our situation here and now? .... It is doubtful that God wants us to play 'First Century Semites'" (16-17).

At the same time some in the church are rejecting the restoration principle, a number of current religious leaders are at the door of restoration. Hans Kung, a Roman Catholic, was affirming something close to the restoration principle when he wrote his book *The Church* and used the phrase, *ecclesia semper reformanda*, which translated means, "The church is always reforming" (339).

ATTEMPTS AT RESTORATIONS

Some of the apostolic fathers called for the rejection of false teachings that had corrupted the church and a return to the teachings of the Scripture. Clement of Rome called the Scriptures inspired and a standard of conduct for the faith and practice of the church.

Examples of this position are also found in the post-apostolic age and the medieval period, even before the Protestant Reformation.

The Renaissance in Europe changed the way men thought. It was an awakening from the bondage of medieval culture and the domination of the Roman Catholic Church. It provided an intellectual climate for the Protestant Reformation. The Scriptures were no longer chained to the pulpit but became available to the people. The translation of the Scriptures into the language of the people exposed the depth of apostasy into which the Roman Catholic Church had gone. The printing press was invented, and the Scriptures were printed and distributed, setting the stage for the Protestant Reformation.

Observe that the term used to describe this period is "reformation," not "restoration." The work of the Reformation leaders was to reform the Roman Catholic Church. Martin Luther, John Calvin and Ulrich Zwingli were each the leader of a reform party, and each succeeded in bringing about many reforms. Zwingli restored a cappella singing in worship and the practice of the Lord's Supper. Luther rejected the doctrine of indulgences and the power of the papacy. He broke with the Roman Catholic Church but retained some of its unscriptural teachings, forms and practices such as sprinkling and instrumental music.

As the Roman Catholics were shackled by the pope, the Protestant parties became shackled by their creeds. The reformer's aim was to reform the Roman Catholic Church by the Bible. A restorer's aim is to restore the church of the Bible. Both the reformers and the restorers regarded the Scriptures as authoritative but did not see them the same way.

Some of the Anabaptists or radicals of the Protestant Reformation seemed to have had the spirit of restoration. No doubt some restored the church in some places at some times. Their goal was correct. We are left to guess what they accomplished. Too little is known of them because persecution by the Protestants and the Roman Catholics drove them into the shadows.

It is not uncommon for indigenous churches to spring up based on the Scriptures without being planted by or connected to any other church. Throughout the world, such is happening in the 21st century. Autonomous churches are practicing New Testament Christianity. The Scriptures are their only guide. Their faith and practice are scriptural without having knowledge of or influence from churches in the United States, Africa or India.

Jesus taught that the seed of the kingdom is the Word of God (Luke 8:11). When the Word of God falls into good, honest hearts and is believed and obeyed, it produces Christians. Where Christians are, there is the church. You cannot reproduce a Protestant or a Catholic church from the Scriptures alone. The church portrayed in the New Testament can be reproduced in any age, in any culture, and in any country by following the teachings of the Scriptures. It can be done and has been done.

BACKGROUND OF THE AMERICAN RESTORATION MOVEMENT

John Locke, the English philosopher, wrote in 1689 a document titled "Letter Concerning Toleration." In it he asked:

> But since men are so solicitous about the true church, I would only ask them here, by the way, if it be not more agreeable to the Church of Christ to make the conditions of her communion consist in such things, and such things only, as the

Holy Spirit has in the Holy Scriptures declared, in express words, to be necessary to salvation; I ask, I say, whether this be not more agreeable to the Church of Christ than for men to impose their own inventions and interpretations upon others as if they were of Divine authority, and to establish by ecclesiastical laws, as absolutely necessary to the profession of Christianity, such things as the Holy Scriptures do either not mention, or at least not expressly command?

In the 18th century in Scotland, John Glas, Robert Sandeman, Robert and James Alexander Haldane and Greville Ewing proclaimed the restoration ideal. In 1805, J.A. Haldane, in *Restoration Principle*, affirmed that the New Testament contains instructions concerning every part of worship and conduct of Christian societies, as well as containing the faith and practice of individuals (128-129).

One of the clearest statements of the restoration principle is that given by Alexander Campbell. He contended that the New Testament is a perfect constitution for the worship, discipline and government of the New Testament church and the perfect rule for the particular duties of its members.

Perhaps the best description of the restoration principle would be: "Attempting to following the teachings of Jesus Christ as revealed in the Scriptures both in the lives of individuals and the faith and practice of the church" (DeGroot *The Restoration Principle* 118).

This would mean cutting away doctrines and practices men have absorbed from their cultures, including cutting away human traditions and creeds handed down from the past as well as fads of today. It would also mean adding to the faith and practices all that has been neglected.

NEW TESTAMENT EXAMPLES

Needs for restoration are reflected even in the New Testament. Jesus warned of false teachers who would mislead even the elect (Matthew 24:24). Paul warned the church at Thessalonica of the coming apostasy. The word translated "apostasy" (*apostasia*) literally means "a falling away." In Thessalonica Christians were falling away from the faith that was once for all delivered to the saints (Jude 3). Paul exhorted them to "stand firm and hold to the traditions which you were taught, whether by word of mouth or by letter from us" (2 Thessalonians 2:3, 15).

The church at Ephesus is perhaps the best New Testament example of apostasy. It started with great promise. Twelve men who had received only the baptism of John were converted. Paul preached three months in the synagogue and taught two years in the school of Tyrannus. Luke recorded that "all who lived in Asia heard the word of the Lord, both Jews and Greeks" (Acts 19:10). Priscilla and Aquila stayed there when Paul went to Jerusalem. Apollos was converted there. Luke further notes that "the word of the Lord was growing mightily and prevailing" (v. 20). Sadly, however, things changed.

The dark cloud of apostasy began to appear on the horizon. Paul met the elders of Ephesus at Melitus on his third journey and gave a solemn warning:

> Be on guard for yourselves and for all the flock, among which the Holy Spirit has made you overseers, to shepherd the church of God which He purchased with His own blood. I know that after my departure savage wolves will come in among you, not sparing the flock; and from among your own selves men will arise, speaking perverse things, to draw away the disciples after them. Therefore be on the alert (Acts 20:28-31).

He later wrote a letter to the church at Ephesus exhorting and encouraging them to continue in the Christian walk. They were to stand against and resist the spiritual forces of wickedness and stand firm against the schemes of the devil (Ephesians 6:11-14). They were warned against taking the first step into apostasy by passive neglect.

Paul wrote to Timothy on two occasions while he was at Ephesus. In his first letter, he gave instructions to Timothy to "instruct certain men not to teach strange doctrines" (1 Timothy 1:3). He warned him that "in later times some will fall away from the faith, paying attention to deceitful spirits and doctrines of demons" (4:1).

In Paul's second letter, the apostasy must have grown worse. He instructed Timothy to:

> [P]reach the word; be ready in season and out of season; reprove, rebuke, exhort, with great patience and instructions.

> For the time will come when they will not endure sound
> doctrine; but wanting to have their ears tickled, they will ac-
> cumulate for themselves teachers in accordance to their own
> desires; and will turn away from the truth, and will turn aside
> to myths (2 Timothy 4:2-4.)

By the time Revelation was written, Jesus said that they had left their first love and were to "repent and do the deeds you did at first" (Revelation 2:4-5). They were already in the throes of apostasy and needed to restore the things they were doing when they first became Christians.

The epistles of John are also connected to the church at Ephesus. One of their major purposes was to refute a certain kind of Gnosticism that was leading the church into apostasy. Gnosticism was a fluid religion varying at different times and different places. It was a combination of Greek philosophy, rabbinic Judaism and Eastern mysticism.

John instructed the church at Ephesus instructions about how to deal with false teachings and human innovations. These instructions are a pattern for dealing with apostasy today.

• **First,** do not give fellowship or show hospitality to those who teach a false doctrine:

> Anyone who goes too far and does not abide in the teach-
> ing of Christ, does not have God; the one who abides in the
> teaching, he has both the Father and the Son. If anyone
> comes to you and does not bring this teaching, do not re-
> ceive him into your house, and do not give him a greeting;
> for the one who gives him a greeting participates in his evil
> deeds (2 John 9-11).

Allowing a false teacher to teach a class or preach a sermon is not an act of noble tolerance; it is participation in an evil deed. One must do nothing to encourage or condone a doctrine or a practice that is wrong. Paul predicted that even some of the elders at Ephesus would speak perverse things to draw away disciples after them. He told the church at Rome to "keep your eye on those who cause dissensions and hindrances contrary to the teaching which you learned, and turn away from them" (Romans 16:17). Much of the apostasy affecting the church today could be corrected if those who shepherd the church would watch more carefully those who are given an opportunity to speak from the pulpit and teach in the classroom.

• **Second,** recognize those who teach false doctrine and participate in unscriptural worship practices for what they are – apostates. Some at Ephesus who had been faithful Christians left the fellowship and could not be corrected from their error. Paul identifies them as Hymenaeus and Alexander and tells the church to deliver them to Satan (1 Timothy 1:19-20).

Some at Ephesus had left the church and formed another fellowship. They were not disfellowshiped by the church, but they withdrew their fellowship from the church. What was to be done? John writes: "They went out from us, but they were not really of us; for if they had been of us, they would have remained with us; but they went out, in order that it might be shown that they all are not of us" (1 John 2:19).

Certainly one must not compromise truth to unite with error. Fellowship is a two-way street. One cannot have fellowship with those who refuse fellowship with him. One cannot call someone a brother whom God does not recognize as one of His children. One must not walk with one who refuses to walk with God.

The last letter in the Scriptures that was written to the church at Ephesus was from Jesus Himself. In the letter He wrote:

> But I have this against you, that you have left your first love. Remember therefore from where you have fallen, and repent and do the deeds you did at first; or else I am coming to you, and will remove your lampstand out of its place – unless you repent (Revelation 2:4-5).

The church in Ephesus was in apostasy. They had left their first love and had fallen away. The church was told to repent from the state into which it had fallen and "do the deeds you did at first." Go back to the beginning. That is, stop doing the things that are wrong and begin doing the things that are right. The church then was given a warning. If they did not repent, their lampstand would be removed. They would no longer be the church. They needed restoration!

RESTORATION AND SCRIPTURES

The restoration principle cannot be separated from the inspiration and authority of the Scriptures. They are the standard of authority Jesus and His apostles used in their teachings. They are the standard of authority for testing the truthfulness of a doctrine (Acts 17:11). They contain the pattern of conduct to be followed in all of the churches (1 Corinthians 4:16-17; 2 Thessalonians 2:15). They will be the standard by which a person will be judged on the last day (John 12:48; James 2:12). They are the standard for all that is believed about God, Christ and the Holy Spirit. All that is to be believed and practiced in moral and ethical conduct is to be found in the Scriptures. All that is to be believed and practiced in the work and worship of the church is to be found in the Scriptures.

A re-discovery of these facts motivated all who, throughout the years, have sought to go back to the Scriptures to discover the way God wants men to be, to believe and to act. The American Restoration Movement was such a time. Those who walked in darkness were seeking the light of God's revelation. Their purpose was made clear in their mottos:

- Speak where the Bible speaks and be silent where the Bible is silent.

- Have a "thus saith the Lord" for all we believe and practice.

- Call Bible things by Bible names, and do Bible things in Bible ways.

- In matters of faith, unity; in matters of opinion, liberty; in all things charity.

CHRISTIANS ONLY

The American Restoration Movement has often been described as a unity movement. It was and still is. This unity is to be found in following the teachings of the Scriptures. The very thing that the early restoration leaders opposed was unification by following the traditions of men, the creeds of men and the ecclesiastical authorities. The song from the American Restoration Movement "Do All in the Name of the Lord" by Austin Taylor reflects this sentiment.

What-e'er you do in word or deed,
Do all in the name of the Lord;
Do naught in name of man or creed,
Do all in the name of the Lord.

Be not deceived by worldly greed,
Do all in the name of the Lord;
The Spirit says "in word or deed,"
Do all in the name of the Lord.

Till toils and labors here are done,
Do all in the name of the Lord;
Dear Christian friends, if you'd be one,
Do all in the name of the Lord.

In word or deed, as God decreed,
Do all in the name of the Lord.

FOR DISCUSSION

1. Why do people claiming to follow the Bible not agree in doctrine and practice?

2. How does the devil's use of Scripture in the temptation of Christ serve as a warning to us in our lives?

3. How would you define the restoration principle? Is it valid today? Is there any circumstance in which it would not be valid?

4. What problems arise with trying to restore the church of the early 20th century or of the 19th century?

5. How can the restoration principle be an aid to evangelism?

6. Was the first century church perfect? Is its replication the goal of the restoration principle?

CHAPTER 11

ROAD OF
APOSTASY

R estoration is always preceded by apostasy. Restoration would not be necessary had there not been the falling away of apostasy. The Scriptures reveal that in every age some departed from the will of God and some returned to the will of God.

Adam and Eve refused to follow God's word and were driven from the Garden of Eden. Their second son, Abel, sought to follow the will of God. By faith, he offered a sacrifice that was well pleasing to God and obtained a testimony that he was righteous (Hebrews 11:4). Cain, his brother, was angry because his sacrifice was not acceptable to God. In anger, Cain killed Abel. There was a "falling away" by both Adam and Eve and their first son, Cain. Apostasy soon dominated the world. It became so evil that the Scriptures record: "Then the Lord saw that the wickedness of man was great on the earth, and that every intent of the thoughts of his heart was only evil continually" (Genesis 6:5).

The world of Noah had gone into apostasy. God destroyed the world with the flood, and only Noah, a righteous man, and his family were spared. God made a covenant with Noah and his family by putting the rainbow in the sky as a sign of that covenant. They were to be a righteous remnant.

Soon after, man again "fell away" from the will of God and began to build the tower of Babel to "make for themselves a name" (Genesis 11:4). But they did not finish it because God confused their language, and they scattered over the face of the earth.

PATRIARCHAL PERIOD

God chose Abraham, while living in the midst of pagan idolatry, to become a righteous remnant. His faith was tested over and over again, but he remained true to God. Concerning God's choice of Abraham, the Scriptures say: "For I have chosen him, in order that he may command his children and his household after him to keep the way of the Lord by doing righteousness and justice" (Genesis 18:19).

Wickedness upon the earth continued to increase. Sodom and Gomorrah were so wicked that God destroyed them with fire and brimstone; only Lot and his two daughters were spared. Abraham and his family followed the will of God and became a righteous remnant.

Through the influence of Joseph, the great-grandson of Abraham, the children of Israel came to Egypt to escape a famine. They were honored by the pharaoh and given the land of Goshen. A different pharaoh arose who put the children of Israel in bondage. They became entangled in the culture and began worshiping the gods of Egypt. They fell victim to apostasy.

MOSAIC PERIOD

God empowered Moses to lead the Israelites out of Egypt. They escaped Egypt by following God's command to put the blood of a lamb on the doorposts of their houses. This event was remembered by the Jews at the feast of the Passover. They crossed the Red Sea on dry land and escaped the army of the Egyptians by miracles God performed through Moses. They were to become a righteous remnant.

God gave Moses a law on Mount Sinai to be a standard of righteousness. The rainbow in the sky, the covenant of circumcision, the blood of the Passover lamb were now superseded by the Ten Commandments written by the hand of God on tables of stone. Added to the Ten Commandments were the Mosaic laws concerning worship, government, morality and ethical conduct. During the wilderness wanderings, times of disobedience, grumbling and open rebellion against these God-given laws became the standard conduct. It still remained the absolute standard for their faith and conduct because it was the Word of God. Moses reiterated the law on the plains of Moab before Israel crossed the Jordan River into Canaan. Joshua had it written on an altar of uncut stones in the sight of the people after their victory at Ai. He read all that was written in the law before all the assembly of Israel. It was their standard of faith and practice and the basis for restoration when Israel would apostatize.

It was a God-given, holy law and the absolute standard by which all things were to be judged. The writer of Hebrews tells of the awesome terror that filled the hearts of the people at Sinai when it was given:

> For you have not come to a mountain that may be touched and to a blazing fire, and to darkness and gloom and whirlwind, and to the blast of a trumpet and the sound of words which sound was such that those who heard begged that no further word should be spoken to them. For they could not bear the command, "If even a beast touches the mountain, it will be stoned." And so terrible was the sight, that Moses said, "I am full of fear and trembling" (Hebrews 12:18-21).

The sight was so overwhelming that even Moses, who had the courage to stand before the pharaoh and demand freedom for his people and boldly lead Israel over the dry bed of the Red Sea with a wall of water on either side, was full of fear and trembling. The writer of Hebrews uses this event to show the importance of adhering to the authority of Jesus and adds: "See to it that you do not refuse him who is speaking. For if those did not escape when they refused him who warned them on earth, much less shall we escape who turn away from Him who warns from heaven" (Hebrews 12:25).

PERIOD OF THE JUDGES

During the period of the judges of Israel, assimilation of the religions practiced by the inhabitants of Canaan became a major problem. Over and over Israel forgot God and worshiped idols following the religious practices of the culture. A summary statement is given in the last verse of the book of Judges: "In those days there was no king in Israel; everyone did what was right in his own eyes" (Judges 21:25).

Over and over they went through periods of rebellion against the will of God. God would then punish Israel by bondage, hunger and slave labor. This punishment would cause them to repent and cry out to the Lord in their distress. Finally by the loving kindness of God, they were restored.

Psalm 107 tells of this pattern of conduct in a song. Four times the pattern of apostasy and restoration is repeated but in different contexts:

> There were those who dwelt in darkness and in the shadow
> of death,
> Prisoners in misery and chains,
> Because they had rebelled against the words of God,
> And spurned the counsel of the Most High,
> Therefore He humbled their heart with labor;
> They stumbled and there was none to help.
> Then they cried out to the Lord in their trouble;
> He saved them out of their distresses.
> He brought them out of darkness and the shadow of death,
> And broke their bands apart.
> Let them give thanks to the Lord for His lovingkindness,
> And for His wonders to the sons of men! (Psalm 107:10-15).

PERIOD OF THE KINGS

The same pattern of rebellion, repentance and restoration continued during the period of the kings. This pattern is shown in an event that took place during the reign of Josiah, king of Judah.

In the 18th year of his reign, he ordered the repair of the house of the Lord. During the repairing of the temple, Hilkiah, the high priest, found the book of the law. It had been lost in the place where it should have been read and revered. Its absence had caused Israel to drift into apostasy. Its commands had been disobeyed, and its teachings had been forgotten.

Shaphan, the scribe, read the book of the law to the king. It revealed the will of God that had been neglected and forgotten by Israel. When the king heard the reading of the book of the law, he responded by tearing his clothes in anguish. He knew the judgment of God was upon him and his people because of their neglect of the law of God. He regarded the book of the law as inspired and authoritative. The text says:

> And the king stood by the pillar and made a covenant before the Lord, to walk after the Lord, and to keep His commandments, and His testimonies and His statutes with all his heart and all his soul, to carry out the words of the covenant that were written in this book. And all the people entered into the covenant (2 Kings 23:3).

Reading the book of the law led to a restoration in Israel. Idols were destroyed, false priests rejected, mediums and spiritualists removed. The Passover feast was observed for the first time in many years. The Scriptures record:

> Then the king commanded all the people saying, "Celebrate the Passover to the Lord your God as it is written in this book of the covenant." Surely such a Passover had not been celebrated from the days of the judges who judged Israel, nor in all the days of the kings of Israel and of the kings of Judah (2 Kings 23:21-22).

Josiah led a great restoration. When the book of the law was read, he listened to its teaching and applied it to his own situation. On one hand, this discovery caused him to stop some religious practices that were beyond what the text said. On the other hand, it caused him to start practicing the religious practices that had been ignored or neglected. He saw the importance of obeying what the Scriptures taught and refusing what the Scriptures did not authorize. Because of his willingness to be led by the Word of God, it was said of him: "And before him there was no king like him who turned to the Lord with all his heart and with all his soul and with all his might, according to all the law of Moses; nor did any like him arise after him" (2 Kings 23:25).

Rejecting or neglecting the Word of God always leads to apostasy. Hearing and obeying the Word of the God leads to restoration.

BABYLONIAN CAPTIVITY

Nehemiah, Zerubbabel and Ezra led groups of captive Jews from their Babylon captivity back to Jerusalem. Nehemiah led in rebuilding the walls of the city to protect the people from their enemies. Zerubbabel led in rebuilding the temple that allowed the priests and Levites to offer the sacrifices commanded by the Law of Moses. Ezra lead in the restoration of knowledge of the Law of Moses that had been neglected and forgotten. This was possible because the book of the Law of Moses had been preserved even during their 70 years of captivity.

The Jews who returned with Ezra, Nehemiah and Zerubbabel did not know the law. In their captivity, no temple was available where they could offer sacrifices; no feast days like the Passover and the Feast of Tabernacles could be observed; and no holy Sabbath days respected. Most of the generation carried to Babylon had died during the 70 years of captivity. Much had been forgotten even by those who, as children, remembered seeing the city and the temple. What they did remember was in danger of being forgotten. This was expressed by songs they sang by the rivers of Babylon. Psalm 137:4-6 is an example:

> How can we sing the Lord's song
> In a foreign land?
> If I forget you, O Jerusalem,
> May my right hand forget her skill.
> May my tongue cleave to the roof of my mouth,
> If I do not remember you,
> If I do not exalt Jerusalem
> Above my chief joy.

Ezra, a scribe and teacher, knew and taught the book of the law. He called the people together and read the book of the law and had it explained to the people. They regarded it as inspired and authoritative:

> And he read from it before the square which was in front of the Water Gate from early morning until midday, in the presence of men and women, those who could understand; and all the people were attentive to the book of the law. ... And Ezra opened the book in the sight of all the people for he was standing above all the people; and when he opened it, all the people stood up (Nehemiah 8:3, 5).

This brought about a restoration of the worship of Jehovah. Idols were destroyed, the Sabbath was observed, foreigners were excluded from the temple, and tithes were given. They celebrated the Feast of the Tabernacles that had been neglected during the captivity. It was observed because it had been commanded in the book of the Law of Moses.

It is no insignificant thing that when God speaks, the heart of the hearer should know a sense of awe and godly fear. One is in the presence of the almighty God. What God says is so powerful that His word created the universe. What God says is so powerful man was created from the dust of the earth. What God says is so powerful that by His word He will some day destroy the heavens and the earth and judge all men.

The Scriptures provide a basis for restoration. It did so in the days of Moses when the law was given, in the days of Josiah when the book of the law was read before the people, and in the days of Ezra when the book of the law was used to restore the worship of Jehovah in Jerusalem when Israel returned from Babylonian captivity. It can also restore the faith and practice of New Testament Christianity at the beginning of the 21st century.

A time will never come when some will cease to follow the Lord and fall into apostasy. But a time should never come when those who seek to follow the Lord are not involved in perpetual restoration.

FOR DISCUSSION

1. What is the relationship between restoration and apostasy?

2. How does the example of Noah serve as a template for us today?

3. How does God's judgment against the Israelites in the wilderness serve as a warning for Christians?

4. What does the period of the judges in Israel teach us about the cycle of sin and repentance?

5. What lessons concerning false religious leaders can be gathered from the history of the kings of Israel and Judah?

6. How does the Babylonian captivity mirror the condition of the church in the world today?

CHAPTER 12

THE 1889 DIVISION

In an historical sense, members of the church of Christ are heirs of the American Restoration Movement. This fact has been well documented. But if our heritage is not more than that, we are no different from the Mormons or any number of other groups who have historical roots in a movement. What makes us different? We still hold to the ideal of restoring first-century Christianity as reflected in the New Testament. We seek not merely what the leaders of the restoration taught, but we seek what those leaders sought – to be the church of Jesus Christ uncluttered by the teachings and practices of other religions and the current culture. Overshadowing the historical heritage is the scriptural heritage of being true to the plan, pattern and practices revealed in Scripture.

Members of the church of Christ are debtors to those who have gone before us and who caught the vision of restoring the New Testament church of the first century. They broke a trail for others to follow. It is thrilling to read of their diligence and faith. They preached in brush-covered tabernacles, met in schoolhouses, debated those who were in error, disciplined those who taught false doctrine, and sought to share the gospel with the entire world. They were the pioneers of the faith.

These pioneers were mere men and made mistakes, but their vision for restoration remained firm. They had no creed, no ecclesiastical structure and no clergy. Their watchword was to "speak where the Bible speaks and be silent where the Bible is silent."

PROLOGUE TO DIVISION

After a century of rapid growth described by one author as "like a wild fire in wheat stubble," a dark cloud of division appeared on the horizon. It centered on how the Scriptures were to be viewed. Some within the movement began to question inspiration. Others under pressure from the culture soon introduced innovations in the organization and worship of the church without scriptural authority. Division resulted. Many factors contributed to this division, but the underlying cause was a disregard for the inspiration and authority of the Scriptures. This was the consummating reason for the split in the American Restoration Movement in the last decade of the 19th century.

Doctrinal disagreements among men had occurred since the beginning of the movement, but these differences were resolved through Bible study. This all changed in 1889.

Some wanted to change from the standard of "thus saith the Lord" to a more popular standard of "what appeals to the culture." Instead of a pious faith seeking the will of God, some were listening to the devil's temptation to do their own thing. An ever-growing crescendo toward digression had built for many years, but the events of 1889 brought the crisis to a resounding conclusion.

In February 1889, The National Benevolent Association opened the first home for children. Throughout 1889, every issue of the *Gospel Advocate* discussed such topics as the spiritual leadership of women, instrumental music, societies and the scope and limits of fellowship.

On Aug. 18, 1889, the "Sand Creek Declaration" was read in Shelby Co., Ill. This marked the split between the a cappella and instrumental churches.

In late 1889, A.I. Myhr traveled to Tennessee to organize the Tennessee State Missionary Society.

On Dec. 7, 1889, in St. Louis, Mo., R.C. Cave preached a sermon denying the inspiration of the Scriptures, the virgin birth, the resurrection and water baptism.

Because of these events, 1889 can be identified as the date of the theological division in the American Restoration Movement, although the institutional division was not clearly defined until 1906. Other influences contributed to the split such as tensions between the North and South after the Civil War, social and economic issues between the rich and poor, the urban and rural, and the teachings of college professors influenced by German higher criticism. In 1906, the U.S. Religious Census recognized the difference in the Disciples Church and churches of Christ.

SEGMENTS OF THE DIVISION

The American Restoration Movement ultimately split into three groups, depending on views of the Scriptures. The Disciples of Christ held to a low view of the Scriptures as reflected in the schools. The Independent Christian Church held to the permissive silence of the Scriptures, allowing anything not specifically condemned by the text. Churches of Christ held to a higher view of the Scriptures, considering the silence of the Scriptures as prohibitive.

The different views of the Scriptures, more than any other factor, prompted the division and determined the historical road each group would take in the 20th century.

The future of any religious group is determined by what the members accept as religious authority. Their view of the Scriptures led the Disciples down the road to ecumenical oblivion. Their view of the Scriptures allowed non-biblical innovations to be added to the work and worship of the Independent Christian Church. Their view of the Scriptures led the churches of Christ to "speak where the Bible speaks and be silent where the Bible is silent."

The divergent views of the Scriptures destroyed the unity of the American Restoration Movement at the beginning of the 20th century. It can do the same thing among churches of Christ at the beginning of the 21st century. Those who refuse to learn from history are destined to repeat it.

By 1889, a change of paradigm was recognized within the American Restoration Movement. Some of the church leaders had studied under or had been influenced by German theologians who espoused what was called "higher criticism." This resulted in a low view of the inspiration and the authority of the Scriptures. Professors in the Bible colleges taught it to their students who were soon to fill the pulpits, who in turn taught in the churches where they preached, resulting in a widespread apostasy from the Word of God. One hundred years later, in 1999, Tom Olbright read a paper in the Scholars' Forum at Abilene Christian University noting a change of paradigm among some leaders of churches of Christ. Time has confirmed this observation.

With the change in the view of the Scriptures in 1889, those wanting to promote unscriptural innovations into the work and worship of the church did not believe it was necessary to have scriptural authority to support their views. They were free to accept the religious fads of the culture. They followed the path of Jeroboam who introduced religious changes he "devised in his own heart" (1 Kings 12:33).

The sermon preached in 1889 by R.C. Cave reflected what a large part of the brotherhood was thinking. Already many of the church leaders doubted the inspiration and authority of the Scriptures but were not vocal about it. Cave's sermon was a call for those to come out of the closet and declare their doubts. Cave's sermon was published in a number of papers and spread through the churches. Schools quickly took the side of the digressives. Congregations began to split with the majority of the schools, the papers, the big city churches and the societies going with the Disciples.

In August 1889, Daniel Sommer, editor of the *Octographic Review*, spoke before a large gathering of Christians in Sand Creek, Ill. After he spoke, P.P. Warren read a document called the "Address and Declaration." It acknowledged a clear-cut division between those who used instrumental music and those who sang a cappella. It read:

> There are among us those who do teach and practice things not taught or found in the New Testament, which have been received by many well-meaning disciples, but rejected by those more thoughtful, and in most instances, better informed in the Scriptures. ... Some of the things of which we hereby complain, and against which we protest, are the unlawful methods resorted to in order to raise or get money for religious purposes; ... the use of instrumental music in the worship; the select choir, ... the man-made society for mis-

sionary work and the one-man, imported preacher pastor to
feed and watch over the flock (Murch 216).

The document closes with this statement, "[I]f they will not turn
away from such abominations, that we can not and will not regard them
as brethren."

The Christian schools quickly embraced the new teachings espoused
by Cave. By 1906, the work at the University of Chicago, the University
of Kentucky, Texas Christian University and a majority of the other
schools were under the control of the Disciples.

Significantly the Childer's Classical Institute was founded in 1906
during the height of the division. Those who founded this institution,
later known as Abilene Christian University, inscribed on its buildings
these affirmations:

> We believe in the Divinity of Christ and the inspiration of
> the Holy Scriptures – contend earnestly for the faith once
> for all delivered to the saints. If you abide in my word then
> are you truly my disciples.You shall know the truth and the
> truth shall make you free.

The language of Abilene Christian University's original charter reflects evidence of the division that had taken place in the American
Restoration Movement. The founders sought to prevent their proper-
ty being taken over by those who no longer held to the restoration principles. The qualifications of the board members are clearly stated:

> Each of whom shall be a member of a congregation of the
> Church of Christ, which takes the New Testament as its only
> and sufficient rule of faith, worship and practice, and rejects
> everything not required by either precedent or example, and
> which does not introduce into the faith, worship and prac-
> tice as a part of the same or adjuncts thereto any supple-
> mental organization or anything else not clearly and directly
> authorized in the New Testament either by precept or ex-
> ample (Cosgrove 12).

In a real sense it can be said that the split in the American Restoration
Movement was not caused by instrumental music, missionary soci-

eties or open fellowship but rather from a view of the Scriptures which allowed these things.

DECISION TIME

In many ways the churches of Christ at the beginning of the 21st century are standing at the same place as their spiritual ancestors did at the beginning of the 20th century. It is decision time. Members of the church of Christ must decide if they are going to take the well-beaten road of apostasy or the high road of restoration. The end of the road for those who go into apostasy is described by Jude: "[C]louds without water, carried along by winds; autumn trees without fruit, doubly dead, uprooted; wild waves of the sea, casting up their own shame like foam; wandering stars, for whom the black darkness has been reserved forever" (Jude 12-13).

The road of apostasy has four turns. Apostasy does not happen all at once but is a process of making decisions leading gradually to digression.

• *First,* there is the hesitancy of standing up for what one believes. Paul said, "I believed, therefore I spoke" (2 Corinthians 4:13). If one believes in the one faith that was once for all delivered to the saints, he should contend for it.

• *Second,* there is a temptation to be tolerant of sin and error. Toleration soon turns into acceptance. Paul admonished those who were extending fellowship to the ones involved in immorality and idolatry to "come out from their midst and be separate" (2 Corinthians 6:16).

• *Third,* toleration turns into association; association turns into participation; participation turns into acceptance. What was first considered to be error has now been accepted as truth. Toleration and association with error bring delusions that allow one to believe what is false (2 Thessalonians 2:11-12).

• *Fourth,* one finds himself affirming and defending error he once vehemently opposed. How sad to see strong leaders in the church who once stood boldly for the truth now despising their roots and ridiculing the faith they once believed. Jude described them as "grumblers, finding fault, following after their own lusts; they speak arrogantly, flattering people for the sake of gaining an advantage" (Jude 16).

WAYS TO AVOID APOSTASY

Negative thinkers will always predict a doomsday for the church. They have what is called a "crisis obsession." They see things as bad and getting worse. They fail to understand that false teachers and church splitters will always seek to deceive the hearts of the faithful. The Lord, in every generation, will be removing the lampstand of some congregations because of apostasy. The current situation is even more serious. A whole group of so-called church leaders now have an agenda to change the church and bring it into conformity with the current culture. Already scores of once faithful gospel preachers are affiliated with the denominations of men. Already former churches of Christ have changed their identity so as not to be associated with what they call "Church of Christ theology."

A general apostasy need not come. Men need to arise to oppose error and affirm truth. The Scriptures, not culture, must be followed as religious authority. Five ways offer direction to avoid the road to apostasy and to walk the high road of restoration.

• *First,* know who you are. One needs to have a strong sense of identity. The church needs to be seen as the family of God, the church of Christ, and the temple of the Holy Spirit. She is the eternal plan of God, purchased by the blood of Jesus and indwelt by the Holy Spirit. The church does not save anyone, but all of the saved are in the church.

The church is not: (1) a protestant church started by Alexander Campbell; (2) a denomination evolving from the American Restoration Movement; (3) a sect appealing to the rural, uneducated, poor segments of society. If any of these descriptions were true, one would not want to be a part of it. Those who would humanize the church enjoy ridiculing the church from which they have fallen away in order to justify their apostasy.

• *Second,* to avoid apostasy have confidence in the gospel message. If the world is not lost, there is no need of proclaiming the gospel. If Jesus is not the Son of God, there is no gospel to proclaim. If the Scriptures are not complete and true, then there is no valid record of who Jesus is or what He taught. Those on the road of restoration have a message to share. Those on the road of apostasy preach only gloom and doom in the church. Secular means of institutional growth are the goals of those on the road to apostasy rather than preaching the good news of Jesus Christ.

• ***Third,*** seek to restore New Testament Christianity. Some have given up on restoration. Those who reject restoration are on the road of apostasy. They do not believe restoration is possible, and if it were they would not want to be a part of it. They refuse to take seriously the exhortation of Paul: "So then, brethren, stand firm and hold to the traditions which you were taught, whether by word of mouth or by letter from us" (2 Thessalonians 2:15).

Without a scriptural pattern, the church of the 21st century will become like Israel in the days of the judges: "Every man doing right in his own eyes."

• ***Fourth,*** to avoid apostasy have watchful leaders. The elders of the church at Ephesus were exhorted to "watch" and "be alert." The devil knows how to place false leaders into the vacuum left by those who are supposed to lead but refuse to do so (Acts 20:30-31). Leaders are to test the spirits whether they are from God (1 John 4:1). The church is not to give fellowship to false teachers (2 John 9-11).

Leaders are needed to cut through the maze of human traditions and return to the Scriptures. Leaders are needed who are not influenced by cultural allurements but who will stand fast on the teachings of the Scriptures. Leaders are needed who will not be swayed by emotional experiences but who know the will of God and have the faith to uphold it.

• ***Fifth,*** the church must practice discipline if it is going to avoid apostasy. The road to apostasy is cluttered with lost souls who could have been saved by corrective discipline. To think of church discipline as negative, judgmental and unloving is a mistake. It is just the opposite. Discipline is a positive step taken by the church to bring about a positive result – that of saving souls. It is not judgmental. It is taking the objective Word of God and comparing it with the objective conduct of a person. If the two contradict, then the judgment of God and not man must prevail. It is not hateful but rather the flip side of love. The Scriptures says: "Whom the Lord loves He disciplines" (Hebrews 12:6).

Immoral persons in the church must be disciplined. Without discipline, the immorality will spread (1 Corinthians 5:5-7).

Divisive persons in the church must be disciplined (Roman 16:17-18).

Many church divisions could have been avoided if the divisive people who led them had been disciplined before gaining a following.

The church must acknowledge those who have left the fellowship (1 John 2:19). You cannot withdraw fellowship from one who is not in fellowship, but the departure from the fellowship needs to be acknowledged.

History tells us that most churches we read about in the New Testament took the road of apostasy. Some people still living remember the trauma resulting when most churches of Christ involved in the American Restoration Movement took the road of apostasy at the turn of the 20th century. This tragedy must not be repeated by the churches of Christ at the beginning of the 21st century.

FOR DISCUSSION

1. Why is 1906 looked upon as the dividing line between the Christian Church and the churches of Christ? In what ways is 1889 a more realistic date to consider as the point of division than 1906?

2. What were the reasons for the division of churches of Christ and the Christian Church? Were these reasons valid then, and are they still valid today?

3. The wording of Abilene Christian University's original charter was very restrictive. Was this appropriate, and has this same outlook been maintained at Christian colleges currently?

4. How have youth and campus ministries contributed to apostasy? How can these works of the church be used to prevent apostasy?

5. What do you think is the greatest doctrinal danger facing the churches of Christ today?

CHAPTER 13

NEW CHALLENGES FACING THE CHURCH

Sacrifices were still being offered in the temple during the time of Jesus. The Torah was being read in the synagogues. Rabbis and scribes searched the Scriptures diligently, but Jesus said: "You search the Scriptures, because you think that in them you have eternal life; and it is these that bear witness of Me" (John 5:39).

They were scholars, but their view of the Scriptures was such that they missed the main point. They missed the witness of the Scriptures to the coming Messiah. Their different views of the Scriptures caused them to form religious parties.

The Pharisees were legalists who put their own interpretations of the Scriptures on the same level as the Scriptures themselves. They built a fence around the law with their traditions. Jesus said that they made void the commandments of God with their human traditions (Matthew 15:6).

The Sadducees were agnostics who rejected parts of the Scriptures. They did not believe in angels or spirits (Acts 23:8). John said the Gnostics regarded their own illuminations to be above the Scriptures (1 John 2:4). John warned his readers not to "believe every spirit, but test the spirits to see whether they are from God" (4:1).

The Herodians compromised the Scriptures with Greek culture for political purposes. Their view of the Scriptures enabled them to make such compromises.

The Essenes were a monastic party who withdrew from the world to live in isolation. They developed rules of conduct beyond what the Scriptures taught. All members of the group were required to follow these rules.

The Zealots were a radical group opposed to the Roman rule. Their faith was more political than religious.

Each of these groups had presuppositions about the nature of the Scriptures and the ways to interpret them. Their views caused party divisions and a perversion of the text then just as it does now.

HANDLING ACCURATELY THE WORD OF TRUTH

Timothy was admonished to handle "accurately the word of truth" (2 Timothy 2:15). The variety of ways to view the Scriptures will lead to apostasy if they are not handled accurately.

1. They can be rejected as being uninspired.
2. They can be spiritualized to mean what any one wants them to mean.
3. They can be contaminated with the traditions of men.
4. They can be accepted in part and rejected in part.
5. They can be added to or taken away from to conform to what one wants to believe.

Generally, the rejection of the inspiration and authority of the Scriptures is an unreasoned silent decision of a person's will. Because he does not want to believe, he seeks a reason for his unbelief.

The cause of rejecting the Scriptures may also include a spirit of apathy. If one does not stand up for truth or speak out against error, he does not take his faith seriously. His faith has become a traditional faith, a convenient faith, a culturally popular faith or a compromised faith. It is faith without conviction. James calls it a dead faith (James 2:26).

Several issues facing the church today are very near to the issues causing the apostasy of the church at the turn of the 20th century.

1. An organizational change: Mission and benevolent societies outside the church were doing the work of the church.

2. A worship change: Instrumental music was added or substituted for worshiping God in song.
3. A leadership change: Women's leadership in the church was sanctioned and practiced.
4. An identity change: Fellowship was broadened to include those in denominations.

Underlying this apostasy was a changing view of the Scriptures as reflected in Cave's sermon in St. Louis denying inspiration. This changing view of the Scriptures allowed the use of instrumental music in worship which the Scriptures do not authorize. The purpose of worship in song was ignored. Worship is to express, not to impress. Worship in song in the New Testament church was expressing praise from the heart with the spirit and with understanding. It was not to impress the pagans with a musical performance but to praise God and edify one another. Worship is something you do, not something done to you or for you. It is expression, not impression.

FAITH CHALLENGES

Five challenges face leaders of the church at the beginning of the 21st century. These challenges arise from one's view of the Scriptures. Either the Scriptures are inspired and authoritative, or they are of human origin, permissive and accommodating to the culture. How one views the Scriptures reflects whether he or she is traveling the high road to restoration or the well-beaten path to apostasy.

• **First,** the changing view of Scripture allows the practice of things that God does not command. Forgotten is the story of Nadab and Abihu, sons of Aaron. They substituted strange fire in their censors "which He had not commanded them." God was not pleased and sent fire from heaven to consume them (Leviticus 10:1ff).

God spoke to Israel through Jeremiah concerning the offering of their children as a sacrifice to Baal. He said it was "a thing which [He] never commanded or spoke of, nor did it ever enter [His] mind" (Jeremiah 19:5). Moses condemned those prophets who presumptuously spoke words that God had not commanded (Deuteronomy 18:20-21). It was and is the sin of presumption to speak what God has not commanded. God warned Israel through Moses to "observe to do just as the Lord your

God has commanded you; you shall not turn aside to the right or to the left" (5:32). Paul speaks of the same principle: "And whatever you do in word or deed, do all in the name of the Lord" (Colossians 3:17).

The changing view of Scripture presumes upon the silence of the Scriptures. Those who hold this view say that this allows anything the Scriptures do not explicitly condemn. How one regards the silence of the Scriptures illustrates the interpretation used by those who desire to sprinkle babies, use instrumental music or change the elements and time of observing the Lord's Supper.

Some are saying that if the Scriptures are silent about a doctrine or a practice it is all right to believe it or to practice it. This is permissive silence. This understanding allows anything not expressly forbidden in Scripture. Fried chicken and Dr. Pepper would be acceptable to eat and drink in observing the Lord's Supper. The Scripture does not say that such a substitute is wrong. However the silence of the Scriptures does not allow it. No command, example or necessary inference would authorize such a change or addition to the New Testament practice of the "fruit of the vine" (Matthew 26:29).

If the Scriptures are silent about a doctrine or practice, then one must not teach it or practice it. This is prohibitive silence. Unleavened bread and grape juice are to be used in the Lord's Supper and nothing else. Jesus used these elements in instituting the Lord's Supper (Matthew 26:26-29). Paul taught that these same elements were to be used in his letter to Corinth (1 Corinthians 11: 23-25). To suggest that other elements could be used is presumptuous. One is to have a "thus saith the Lord for all that is believed and practiced." The silence of the Scriptures prohibits adding any teaching or practice not authorized in Scripture.

Jesus understood the silence of the Scriptures to be prohibitive. He demonstrated this by His response to the temptations of the devil. When Satan promised Him all the kingdoms of the earth if He would fall down and worship him, Jesus replied: "For it is written, 'You shall worship the Lord your God, and serve Him only.'" Jesus quoted Deuteronomy 6:13 but added His own commentary by adding the word "only." The word "only" is not in the Hebrew text. Jesus understood the silence of the text to exclude all who were not contained in it. He did not have to mention all the gods of Egypt, Canaan and Babylon. Worshiping "the Lord your God" excluded all of these.

If you ask a waitress for coffee, she knows not to bring a soft drink, water or tea. If God says to express praise and edification by singing, He excludes instrumental music.

The silence of Scripture prohibits making an innovation that God did not command as part of the faith or practice of the church. The silence of Scripture, however, is permissive in carrying out how a command is to be expedited. An example of this can be found in singing different parts in a song – soprano, alto, tenor or bass. The Scriptures teach that one is to sing in worship. They are silent about what part to sing. Scripture silence is permissive about what part to sing but is prohibitive about playing an instrument or dancing as worship

• **Second,** the changing view of Scriptures is often based on experiential interpretations. These interpretations have different forms, but all rely on a personal, emotional experience to determine the will of God. The Calvinists, the Mormons, the Pentecostals, the charismatics and even some who do not believe the Scriptures are inspired share this view.

The orthodox Calvinists believe in predestination. They contend that God has predestined each person to heaven or hell. They say that God places faith in one's heart and that a person has no choice, no free will. He is predestined to be saved or damned before he was born, and he can do nothing about it. An orthodox Calvinist says that by the miracle of God's intervention in an experiential way one comes to faith and to an understanding of the Scriptures.

The Pentecostals and charismatics believe in the direct intervention of the Holy Spirit on an individual in order for him to be saved. This includes messages from God through speaking in tongues, interpretation of tongues, miracles and prophecies. These experiences, they believe, are on the same level as the Scriptures; they are inspired. The Scriptures themselves are interpreted experientially. These people seek a miraculous revelation to know what the Scriptures mean. They ignore the fact that what they claim is a direct revelation from God might be in direct contradiction to what another person claims to have received from God.

Mormons claim inspiration for the Book of Mormon. Their claim is that if one prays with a sincere heart, God will reveal to him that the

Book of Mormon is inspired. They ask a person to receive an experiential response to such a prayer.

A more sophisticated experiential view for interpreting the Scriptures is espoused by many college professors in universities and seminaries. They follow the explanation of inspiration by Stendahl in *The Bible and the Role of Women*: "Thus we have in the Bible what is absolute only in and through what is relative. It is the work of the Spirit to make the word of man in the Bible into God's absolute word to us" (16).

Inspiration is to be found in the reader or hearer – experientially – rather than in the text.

•*Third,* The changing view of the Scriptures can be found in the rejection of apostolic traditions or as some would say rejecting an approved apostolic example. This view is sometimes called pattern theology and is portrayed as bad hermeneutics by those who reject it. They ignore the fact that the practices of the church as revealed in the New Testament are a part of the way the apostles delivered the teachings of God to man. What they taught by words, they modeled in actions. Their approved apostolic examples were to be followed. The pattern of "all the churches" was used by Paul to teach the quiet submissive conduct for women in the church (1 Corinthians 14:34).

Tradition (*paradosis*) is not always a bad word in Scriptures. It is used for what has been "handed down" from the past or "handed over" from the present. If men pass down the tradition, it is a human tradition. Jesus condemned this kind of tradition as religious authority. Jesus, in confronting the Pharisees who tried to bind this kind of human traditions on the apostles, said, "Why do you yourselves transgress the commandment of God for the sake of your tradition? ... [Y]ou invalidated the word of God for the sake of your tradition" (Matthew 15:3, 6).

Tradition in a good sense in the Scriptures refers to what has been received from God and handed down by the apostolic men who by inspiration wrote the New Testament. These are apostolic traditions. They are inspired teachings or acts and are to be regarded as authoritative.

Paul used a technical literary formula in his letter to show that these apostolic traditions were to be followed. Traditions were received from the Lord and delivered to the church. Two examples of this formula are found in 1 Corinthians.

In teaching the observance of the Lord's Supper, Paul used this literary formula of "received" and "delivered":

> For I received from the Lord that which I also delivered to you, that the Lord Jesus in the night in which He was betrayed took bread; and when He had given thanks, He broke it, and said, "This is My body, which is for you; do this in remembrance of Me" (1 Corinthians 11:23-24).

A teaching of first importance, the death, burial and resurrection of Jesus, was given by this formula of "delivered" and "received":

> For I delivered to you as of first importance what I also received, that Christ died for our sins according to the Scriptures, and that He was buried, and that He was raised on the third day (1 Corinthians 15:3-4).

Inspired words were received from God and delivered to apostles and the other men who wrote the New Testament, and in the same way inspired practices were revealed from God and delivered to the church. Paul made it clear to the Corinthians that what he received from the Lord was to be delivered to His disciples. He wrote the same things to the church at Thessalonica: "So then, brethren, stand firm and hold to the traditions which you were taught, whether by word of mouth or by letter from us. ... [K]eep aloof from every brother who leads an unruly life and not according to the tradition which you received from us" (2 Thessalonians 2:15; 3:6).

He wrote the same kind of exhortation to the church at Philippi: "The things you have learned and received and heard and seen in me, practice these things" (Philippians 4:9).

These passages show that what the apostles spoke, wrote and practiced in the church are to be followed. Noah followed a pattern when he built the ark. Moses followed a pattern when he built the tabernacle. He was instructed to build it "according to the pattern which was shown [him] on the mountain" (Hebrews 8:5; Exodus 25:40).

Not all apostolic examples, however, are to be followed. They must be approved apostolic examples. That is, the text and context must show that the practice or doctrine was approved by apostolic authority.

One need not meet in an upper room of a house located at Troas to observe the Lord's Supper just because Paul did (Acts 20:7). Where they met to observe the Lord Supper was incidental to the Lord's instructions to observe the Lord Supper.

• *Fourth,* the changing view of the Scriptures can be found in adapting the text to culture. The Scriptures, some would say, are not to be regarded as teachings to be taken literally because they were written in an ancient time to a strange culture, and they apply only to those to whom they were originally addressed. They contend that such teaching does not apply in today's world.

Some would say that practices relevant then are not relevant today. The ancient taboo against homosexuality, for example, does not apply. They add that the submissiveness of women to their husbands and in the church does not apply. These teachings are to be understood, they say, as a prejudice of an oppressive society in the first century. It becomes the task of "scholars" to determine what that ancient culture was and how Scripture written at that time is to be interpreted in today's world.

Certainly the Scriptures are to be interpreted in their context. The context however is used to understand the meaning of the text not to change it. The Greek word *"glossa"* can be interpreted as "physical tongue," a "language of man," or an "inspired utterance." The context determines which meaning is to be understood. A fabrication of the context is too often used to find a meaning the interpreter wants to find.

• *Fifth,* the changing view of the Scriptures can be found in those who quote a passage or phrase out of context to prove a point that is totally unrelated to the text. This practice is sometimes called "proof texting." An example would be: "[Judas] went away and hanged himself" (Matthew 27:5). "Jesus said, 'Go and do the same'" (Luke 10:37). That is proof texting in a bad sense. It is Scripture taken out of context to mean something different from it's meaning in context.

Good "proof texting" should be practiced, that is bringing together those passages of Scriptures that teach on a certain subject to better understand the meaning of another passage. One uses proof texting when he brings together passages from the Gospels to give information on the Lord's Supper when he is studying 1 Corinthians 11:20-34. The bringing together of other texts dealing with the same subject brings a better understanding of the meaning of the text. Those who ridicule this kind of proof texting should listen to Luke: "they received the word with great eagerness, examining the Scriptures daily, to see whether these things were so" (Acts 17:11).

CONCLUSION

Historically members of the church of Christ might consider themselves heirs of the American Restoration Movement because they are indebted to those who courageously sought to restore New Testament Christianity in the 19th century. A motto in the office of the Gospel Advocate speaks of how one should regard these leaders today: "I do not seek to follow in the footsteps of the men of old; I seek the things they sought" (Basho).

We are individually the children of God, the disciples of Jesus Christ, and the temple of the Holy Spirit. We are collectively the kingdom of God, the body of Christ, and the dwelling place of the Holy Spirit.

The church that Jesus established can exist wherever and whenever the seed of the Word of God is planted in the hearts of men and obeyed. The Scriptures are God's inspired revelation to man and are to be the only religious authority for faith and conduct.

The American Restoration Movement was one of many attempts to restore New Testament Christianity at a time and place where most who claimed to follow Jesus Christ had apostatized. In the first century of the movement (1806-1889), it was a dynamic force, seeking to discard what was not scriptural and to add to the faith and practices that had been neglected by men. Its goal was not only to reform but to restore the New Testament church in the 19th century.

During the second century of the movement (1889-1989), doubt and compromise brought changes in how the Scriptures were to be viewed. Many in the movement apostatized by rejecting scriptural authority and accepting the permissive silence of the Scriptures to conform to the culture. A remnant still sought to be true to the restoration principle.

At the beginning of the third century, the American Restoration Movement again has pockets of doubt and compromise among those who consider themselves members of the church of Christ. Most of the teachings that shattered the unity of the American Restoration Movement in 1889-1906 are again causing strife and division. Parties are being formed, churches are going into apostasy, false teachers are given liberty to subvert their classes and congregations. And God's children are hiding their heads in the sand.

Now is the time for elders to take heed to themselves and be on the alert for men who teach perverse things. Now is the time for preachers to preach the word even when it does not please those with itching ears. Now is the time for all children of God to renew their restoration zeal, not of the teachings of leaders in the American Restoration Movement, but of the teachings of Jesus Christ as revealed in Scripture.

At the end of the first century, apostasy came to a large portion of the American Restoration Movement. Has the process begun all over again? At the end of the second century of the movement, we are discussing the same issues that divided the American Restoration Movement in 1889. Let us pray that God's children will be firm in the faith and renew their commitment to "speak where the Bible speaks and be silent where the Bible is silent."

For Discussion

1. Why were the factions among the Jews in the first century not united in their view of Scripture? What lessons can we draw from this situation for the church today?

2. How does apathy in the church pave the way for apostasy?

3. What are some unauthorized religious practices entering churches of Christ today? What are the dangers presented by these innovations and how can they be addressed?

4. What is the value of Christian experience in faith development? What are the dangers of relying on experience to determine truth?

5. What is the role of tradition in the church? What are some good and bad aspects of traditions for God's work?

6. How can congregations of the Lord's church make sure their members remain committed to the truth of Scripture?

WORKS CITED

Bainton, Roland H. *Here I Stand, A Life of Martin Luther*. New York: The New American Library of World Literature, Inc., 1960.

Blackman, E.C. *Bible Interpretation*. Philadelphia: Westminster Press, 1957.

Campbell, Alexander. *The Christian System*. Printed by A. Campbell. Pittsburg: Published by Forrester and Campbell, 1839. <http://www.mun.ca/rels/res mov/texts/acampbell/tcs2/TCS 200A.HTM>

Campbell, Thomas. "Declaration and Address." Printed by Brown and Sample at the Office of "The Reporter," 1809. <http://www.mun.ca/ rels/res mov/texts/tcampbell/da/DA-1ST.HTM>

Casey, Michael. "The Origins of the Hermeneutics of the Churches of Christ, Part One: The Reformed Tradition," *Restoration Quarterly*, Vol. 31, No. 2, 1989. <http://www.restorationquarterly.org>

_____. "The Origins of Hermeneutics of the Churches of Christ, Part Two: The Philosophical Background," *Restoration Quarterly*, Vol. 31, No. 4, 1989.

Cosgrove, Owen. *Don Morris*. Ft. Worth, Texas: Star Bible Publications, 1993.

DeGroot, Alford T. *The Restoration Principle*. St. Louis, Mo.: Bethany Press, 1960.

Dyer, Russell L., Tommy F. Haynes and Jeff A. Jenkins, eds. *Redeeming the Times*. Oklahoma City: Clarity Pub., 2004.

Garrison, Windfred Ernest and Alford T. DeGroot. *The Disciples of Christ, A History*. St. Louis, Mo.: Bethany Press, 1948.

Ingersoll, Robert G. *Some Mistakes of Moses*. Buffalo, New York: Prometheus Books, 1986.

Jaspers, Karl and Karl Bultmann. *Myth and Christianity: An Inquiry Into the Possibility of Religion Without Myth*. New York: Noonday Press, 1958.

Kittle, Gerhard and Gerhard Friedrich, eds. *Theological Dictionary of the New Testament*, Vol. V. Grand Rapids, Mich.: Eerdmans, 1973.

Kung, Hans. *The Church*. New York: Sheed and Ward, 1967.

Lindsell, Harold. *The Battle for the Bible*. Grand Rapids, Mich.: Zondervan, 1976.

Locke, John. *The Reasonableness of Christianity*. Chicago: Hebrey Regnery Co., 1965.

Malone, Avon. *The View of Inspiration as Reflected in Select Passages from the Pauline Epistles*. M.A. Thesis, Abilene Christian College, 1974.

McGarvey, J.W. *Biblical Criticism*. Nashville: Gospel Advocate, 1956.

Murch, James DeForest. *Christians Only*. Cincinnati: Standard Publishing, 1962.

Pache, Rene. *The Inspiration and Authority of Scriptures*. Salem, Wis.: Sheffield Publishing Co., 1992.

Richardson, Cyril. *Early Christian Fathers*, Vol. I. Philadelphia: Westminster Press, 1953.

Stendahl, Krister. *The Bible and the Role of Women: A Case Study in Hermeneutics*. Philadelphia: Fortress Press, 1973.

Ward, Roy. "Is the Restoration Principle Valid?" *New Testament Christianity the Message for Modern Man*. Nashville: Christian Family Books, 1965.

Printed in the United States
122413LV00004B/13-15/A

9 780892 255450